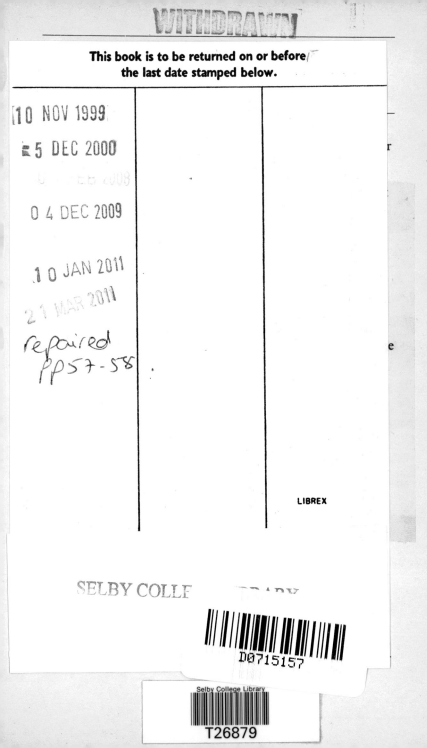

WITHDRAWN

by the same authors

The Classical Monologue (Men and Women)
Soliloquy! The Shakespeare Monologues (Men and Women)
Solo! The Best Monologues of the 80s (Men and Women)

The
Modern Monologue
Men

Edited with notes and commentaries by

MICHAEL EARLEY
& PHILIPPA KEIL

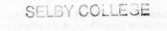
Methuen Drama

First published in Great Britain 1993
by Methuen Drama

7 9 10 8

Random House UK Limited
20 Vauxhall Bridge Road, London SW1V 2SA
and Australia, New Zealand and South Africa

Random House UK Limited Reg. No. 954009

Copyright in the selections, format, introductions and commentaries
© 1993 Michael Earley and Philippa Keil

The editors have asserted their moral rights

ISBN 0–413–67210–7

A CIP catalogue record for this book
is available from the British Library

Typeset by Wilmaset Ltd, Birkenhead, Wirral
Printed and bound in Great Britain by
Cox & Wyman Ltd, Reading, Berkshire

Front cover: Marlon Brando in *A Streetcar Named Desire*
Photo: Warner Bros/The Kobal Collection

Contents

Notes to the Actor

The Modern Monologue is a continuation of our previous collection *The Classical Monologue*. Here we start at the dawn of the modern age in 1892, presenting a survey of indispensable speeches from plays that continue to shape the course of modern theatre. The plays included in this collection also happen to be the ones that have helped to define modern acting in all its many guises.

Modern playwrights such as Brecht, Genet, Beckett, Ionesco, Pinter, Shepard, Guare, Nichols and Churchill, to name only a handful of the dramatists represented here, assume that a play and its characters are malleable and shifting; that mood swings, strangeness and sudden eruptions are key components of modern theatre's compelling attraction. We are, after all, not watching something 'real' but something liberated from reality; not a psychologically whole character but very often an extreme or fragmented one; not life itself but an 'imitation' of life. Theatre is manifestly theatrical. The actor is a partner in this enterprise. His transformational talent makes a key statement about the very nature of modern drama. The modern play provokes the actor to respond freshly to the notion of what it means to be and to perform in front of others.

Modern acting is not just those specific principles formulated by Konstantin Stanislavski and his later followers; principles that relate primarily to realistic and psychologically truthful acting. Like modern drama in all its myriad forms modern acting is full of infinite possibilities. There are as many different styles of acting nowadays as there are actors to fill roles. The plays of this century have been a healthy mixture of realism and anti-realism. The speeches from Alan Ayckbourn's *Absent Friends* and Alfred Jarry's *Ubu* plays, for instance, make completely different demands on the performer. The best modern actors decide approaches to performances according to the unique demands of a role.

In looking at these modern monologues, begin by asking yourself how the speech works and what it demands from you. It may be realistic but also absurd, humorous and then pathetic, static yet suddenly physical. Tempos and pace might undergo a change. The language may be sparse, eloquent or sheer nonsense. The sentences could run-on or be brief and clipped. The speech may have a structure that is simple but ideas and arguments that are dense and complex. The modern monologue challenges the actor repeatedly to shift gears in performance and manoeuvre swiftly from style to style. That is why these speeches continue to be so exhilarating to perform. That is also why they are excellent for auditions and rehearsals. They display all dimensions of an actor's resources and stretch the imagination.

Each monologue's 'Introduction' sets the character and speech in context. In the 'Commentary' that follows the monologue we hunt out some of the clues that will help you to perform the speech better. Our remarks mean to provoke you to think for yourself about the lines, their content and what they are doing. You are free to disagree with our opinions and we hope, in fact, that you will supply your own interpretation of each speech.

At the end of the book a 'Play Source' directs you to published versions of the full texts from which we have selected these monologues. Few of these speeches will make complete sense to you until you have traced the monologue back to its source and read the entire play thoroughly. You must appreciate the whole play before taking on a part.

Michael Earley
Philippa Keil
London 1992

Absent Friends
(1974) Alan Ayckbourn

Act 2. The open-plan living-room of a modern executive-style house. Saturday afternoon.

Colin (30s) works in a bank. Diana invites him to tea with some of his old 'pals' so that they can show their support for him following the recent death by drowning of his fiancée, Carol. Diana and her friends have not seen Colin in three years and had never met Carol. Regardless of his bereavement and grief Colin has come to terms with his tragic loss, and he turns out to be the only cheerful one at the tea party. In great detail, and much to the embarrassed discomfort of everyone, he explains his contented state. He then proceeds to analyse each of his 'pals'. His insensitive frankness proves irritating and self-righteous. Evelyn, who has been particularly terse towards Colin, becomes his target. Meanwhile her husband, John, is out in the garden.

COLIN. You all right, Evelyn?
[EVELYN. Eh?]
Anything the matter? You seem a bit down.
[EVELYN. No. No. No . . .
MARGE. It's just her manner.
DIANA. You get used to it eventually.]
Oh. Do you know something, Evelyn. Now I'm talking off the top of my head now because I've only just met you, I don't really know you – but – I think Paul will back me on this, won't you, Paul – I've always had this knack – gift if you like, I suppose you could call it – for being able to sum people up pretty quickly. Sometimes I've just got to meet them, exchange a few words with them and on occasions, not always but on occasions, I know more about that particular

person than they know about themselves. Now I could be wrong, as I say this is straight off the top but I would say just from the brief time I've had to study you, I would say something's bothering you. Right or wrong?

[EVELYN. Right.]

There you are. Now, I'm going to go a bit further and I warn you I'm going to stick my neck right out now and say one of your worries is John. Right?

[EVELYN. Amazing.]

No, not altogether. You see, I think I know what it is – (*To the others*.) excuse me, I'm just putting Evelyn straight – right. Number one. John is a very high-powered individual – can't sit still, always on the move. We all know him in this room very well. Probably better than you do, Evelyn. You see, we've known him for years. He's an extrovert, good brain, clever – wonderful with his hands. The sort of fellow, if you're in trouble, it's John you go to. John is number one. Never let you down. The bee's knees. But – and there's a big but – and I think everyone here will agree with this – Marge, Di, Paul, Gordon if he was here – what we, everyone of us, have always said about John is – God help the woman he marries. Because every day of their lives together, she is going to have to get used to the fact that John is going to be the driver while she is going to have to spend most of her life in the back seat. (*He pauses for effect and gets one.*) So. My advice is, don't let your personality – because I can see there's a lovely personaiity hiding under there – don't let that get buried away. Because he won't thank you for it in the end. Nobody will. Get in the habit of giving yourself to people. If you know what I mean, and you'll get a lot more back, believe me. I'm a giver. It's natural, how I was born, nothing virtuous about it, *per se* – just the way I'm made. Others have to work at it. Carol was another giver. She'd give you everything. Everything she had. (*Silence.*)

[MARGE. True. True . . .]

2

Sorry. I'm preaching. I can feel it. Sorry, Evelyn. Beg your pardon. I just happen to be an expert on John, that's all. I'm an expert on Paul here as well. Shall I tell you about Paul?

COMMENTARY: *Absent Friends*, like so many of Ayckbourn's best early plays, is a comedy of modern manners. Behind the surface humour is a shrewd analysis of suburban mores, disillusion and despair. Ayckbourn is skilled at creating situations and characters that have both comic and sad elements that reveal the pain of everyday life and blighted relationships. In *Absent Friends* the issues of death and deceit are given a laughable gloss. This is a darkly hilarious play.

What you instantly notice about Colin is his all-embracing friendliness; he has a wonderfully confiding bedside manner especially when he has an audience. He is full of apologies and is endearingly kind. There is something of the lay psychologist about him, and although he means well, he unerringly gets everyone wrong. Late in the speech he identifies himself as a 'giver', a 'preacher'. Colin is infuriatingly slow at getting to the main point of any sentence. Notice how his speech is cluttered with halting, detached clauses that pile up like a landslide. He favours thinking out loud and believes that his listeners are hanging on his every word. Colin is the sort of fellow who makes his listeners lean in so that he can be heard and understood. He gives the impression, too, of being more profound than he actually is. Notice how he babbles on, blithely insensitive to the impact all this is having. Yet what do you make of his feelings about John? What might he say next about Paul? Just how much about these men, and their affairs with other women, does Colin know?

All My Sons

(1947) Arthur Miller

Act 3. The back yard of the Keller home on the outskirts of an American town. Twilight.

George Deever (32) is 'a pale man . . . on the edge of his self-restraint. He speaks quietly, as though afraid to find himself screaming'. He has come to the Keller house for a showdown. During the war his father and Joe Keller were partners in an airplane parts factory. Defective cylinder heads were knowingly shipped to the Air Force, causing the deaths of twenty-one pilots. George's father was found guilty and sent to prison while Joe Keller was exonerated. Larry, one of Keller's two sons, was a pilot and has been declared missing in action. George's sister, Ann had been engaged to Larry, but is now engaged to his brother Chris. George has come from visiting his father in prison with fresh information and the intention of preventing his sister's marriage to Chris Keller. George brings his legal training into play in this speech as he reconstructs the incident for his sister.

GEORGE (*breathlessly*). My life turned upside down since then. I couldn't go back to work when you left. I wanted to go to Dad and tell him you were going to be married. It seemed impossible not to tell him. He loved you so much. (*He pauses.*) Annie – we did a terrible thing. We can never be forgiven. Not even to send him a card at Christmas. I didn't see him once since I got home from the war! Annie, you don't know what was done to that man. You don't know what happened.

[ANN (*afraid*). Of course I know.]

You can't know, you wouldn't be here. Dad came to work that day. The night foreman came to him and showed him

4

the cylinder heads . . . they were coming out of the process with defects. There was something wrong with the process. So Dad went directly to the phone and called here and told Joe to come down right away. But the morning passed. No sign of Joe. So Dad called again. By this time he had over a hundred defectives. The Army was screaming for stuff and Dad didn't have anything to ship. So Joe told him . . . on the phone he told him to weld, cover up the cracks in any way he could, and ship them out.

[CHRIS. Are you through now?]

(*Surging up at him.*) I'm not through now! (*Back to* ANN.) Dad was afraid. He wanted Joe there if he was going to do it. But Joe can't come down. . . . He's sick. Sick! He suddenly gets the flu! Suddenly! But he promised to take responsibility. Do you understand what I'm saying? On the telephone you can't have responsibility! In a court you can always deny a phone call and that's exactly what he did. They knew he was a liar the first time, but in the appeal they believed that rotten lie and now Joe is a big shot and your father is the patsy. (*He gets up.*) Now what're you going to do? Eat his food, sleep in his bed? Answer me; what're you going to do?

COMMENTARY: Arthur Miller's *All My Sons* is a tightly woven and powerful domestic drama. It was Miller's first stage success and remains one of his most popular and often performed plays. The drama contains a clear, timeless moral message: we are all responsible to and for each other; the sins of the father must be expiated by the children. You cannot help but be aware of the influence of classical Greek tragedy and Ibsen's drama on this play as it explores the conflict between individual greed and social responsibility.

When George Deever enters the closed world of the Keller household, he arrives as a truth seeker, an avenging angel. He is a man in search of justice and a culprit: Joe Keller. Most of all he is a son trying to clear the sullied reputation of his father who has been framed, tried and imprisoned for a crime he did not commit. In this speech, which tumbles out of George 'breathlessly' (he has waited for three long acts to deliver it), he finally gets to speak his mind. Love, hate, rejection, terror, filial duty and brotherly love are woven together into a confusing and combustible mix. The actor must open himself to the warring contradictions of all these competing emotions. Like a lawyer in front of a jury, George displays the horrifying facts. Each one is laid before his sister in a step by step suspenseful chronology of their father's downfall. The defective cylinder heads are synonymous with the smoking pistol in a crime drama. The speech falls into three parts with two interruptions. George is speaking to his sister Ann and to his adversary Chris. So you have to make both these other characters, close to you as family and friend, part of the scene. For the actor the thrill of this speech is that the suspense builds and ends with a moral challenge and a question.

American Buffalo
(1975) David Mamet

Act 1. Don's resale shop. A junk shop in Chicago. One Friday morning.

Teach (30s) is a small-time crook. Don, one of his partners, runs a second-hand shop, and the play opens with him and Bob talking 'business'; they are planning to steal a coin collection. Teach enters after a couple of minutes and launches into this speech.

TEACH (*walks around the store a bit in silence*). Fuckin' Ruthie, fuckin' Ruthie, fuckin' Ruthie, fuckin' Ruthie, fuckin' Ruthie.
[DON. What?]
Fuckin' *Ruthie* . . .
[DON. . . . yeah?]
I come into the Riverside to get a cup of *coffee*, right? I sit down at the table Grace and Ruthie.
[DON. Yeah.]
I'm gonna order just a cup of coffee.
[DON. Right.]
So Grace and Ruthie's having breakfast, and they're done. *Plates* . . . *crusts* of stuff all over . . . So we'll shoot the shit.
[DON. Yeah.]
Talk about the *game* . . .
[DON. . . . yeah.]
. . . *so* on. Down I sit. 'Hi, hi.' I take a piece of toast off Grace's plate . . .
[DON. . . . uh-huh . . .]
. . . and she goes 'Help yourself.' Help myself. I should

7

help myself to half a piece of toast it's four slices for a quarter. I should have a nickel every time we're over at the game, I pop for coffee . . . cigarettes . . . a *sweet* roll, never say word. 'Bobby, see who want what.' Huh? A fucking *roast-beef* sandwich. (*To* BOB.) Am I right? (*To* DON.) Ahh, shit. We're sitting down, how many times do I pick up the check? But (No!) because I never go and make a big *thing* out of it – it's no big thing – and flaunt like 'This one's on me' like some bust-out asshole, but I naturally assume that I'm with friends, and don't forget who's who when someone gets *behind* a half a yard or needs some help with (huh?) some fucking rent, or drops enormous piles of money at the track, or someone's *sick* or something . . .

[DON (*to* BOB). This is what I'm talking about.]

Only (and I tell you this, Don). Only, and I'm not, I don't think, casting anything on anyone: from the mouth of a Southern bulldyke asshole ingrate of a vicious nowhere cunt can this trash come. (*To* BOB.) And I take nothing back, and I know you're close with them.

[BOB. With Grace and Ruthie?

TEACH. Yes.

BOB. (I like 'em.)]

I have always treated everybody more than fair, and never gone around complaining. Is this true Don?

[DON. Yup.]

Someone is *against* me, that's their problem . . . I can look out for myself, and I don't got to fuck around behind somebody's back, I don't like the way you're treating me. (Or pray some brick *safe* falls and hits them on the head, they're walking down the street.) But to have that shithead turn, in one breath, every fucking sweet roll that I ever ate with them into *ground glass* (I'm wondering were they eating it and thinking 'This guy's an idiot to blow a fucking *quarter* on his friends' . . .) . . . this hurt me, Don. This hurts me in a way I don't know what the fuck to do.

8

COMMENTARY: *American Buffalo* was the play that launched David Mamet's reputation as one of America's best modern dramatists. It traces the shifting relationships among three small-time criminals, with big ambitions and egos, as they foolishly plan to steal a coin collection of dubious value. The play inhabits a rough urban world with its own code of macho ethics. Mamet's particular skill lies in his ability to write speakable dialogue for actors, capturing the zesty flippant cadence of street-talk. His words come at the audience in a rapid-fire delivery that is riveting even when it is profane. Actors as different as Robert Duvall, Al Pacino and Jack Shepherd have played the central role of Teach.

Teach cannot stand still. Notice that even when he is sitting he is constantly shifting and fidgeting. The words he uses are seismic proof of his body quakes and his eruptive personality. He bursts into the room. All the words have that fragmentary edginess that you usually find in a Mamet speech. Each phrase has to be backed up and punctuated with appropriate body language. The words are projected through gestures and facial contortions. Teach uses profanity and especially the 'F' word to such excess that it must seem comic after a while. The repetition of it, however, can also be used as a pacing and punctuating device in the speech. Teach uses words and street argot with great authority and emphasis. His grasp of both language and reality is highly idiosyncratic. He speaks in codes that have a very precise meaning. These must be clear to the actor or else the speech will seem like nonsense. Respect his idiom and master it. Everybody disgusts him, everybody cheats on him and he in turn slags them off. He also thinks he's more intelligent than everyone around him. But Teach is a man who can easily lose control and fly into a rage.

Antigone
(1944) Jean Anouilh

Scene 1. Set without historical or geographical connotations. Vaguely Greek but more modern.

This speech by the one-man Chorus opens the play and sets the scene, informing the audience of the background of the characters and the action.

PROLOGUE. The people gathered here are about to act the story of Antigone. The one who's going to play the lead is the thin girl sitting there silent. Staring in front of her. Thinking. She's thinking that soon she's going to be Antigone. That she'll suddenly stop being the thin dark girl whose family didn't take her seriously, and rise up alone against everyone. Against Creon, her uncle . . . the king. She's thinking she's going to die . . . though she's still young, and like everyone else would have preferred to live.

But there's nothing to be done. Her name is Antigone, and she's going to have to play her part right through to the end.

Ever since the play started she has felt herself hurtling further and further away from her sister Ismene. (That's her, chatting and laughing with a young man over there.) Further and further away from all the rest of us, who are just here to watch, and haven't got to die in a few hours' time.

The young man talking to Ismene – fair-haired, beautiful, happy Ismene – is Haemon, son of Creon. He is Antigone's fiancé. Everything combined to attract him to Ismene – his love of dancing and sport, of happiness and success. His

10

senses too, for Ismene is much prettier than Antigone. And then one evening, when there was a ball and he'd been dancing every dance with Ismene, dazzling in a new gown, he went and sought out Antigone where she sat dreaming in a corner, as she is now, with her arms clasped round her knees. And he asked her to be his wife. She looked up at him with those sober eyes of hers, unsurprised, smiled a sad little smile . . . and said 'yes'. The orchestra struck up again, Ismene was there across the room, in peals of laughter among the young men . . . and now he, Haemon, was going to be Antigone's husband. He didn't know that never in this world would there be such a person as Antigone's husband. That all this princely title conferred on him was the right to die.

The vigorous grey-haired man deep in thought, his young page beside him, is Creon, the king. He is wrinkled, tired. He is playing a difficult game: he has become a leader of men. Before, in the reign of Oedipus, when Creon was only the most influential man at court, he loved music and fine buildings, would spend hours prowling round Thebes's little antique shops. But Oedipus and his sons are dead. And Creon, forsaking his books and his collector's pieces, has rolled up his sleeves and taken their place. Sometimes, in the evening, when he's worn out, he wonders whether it's not pointless, being a leader of men. Whether it's not a sordid business that ought to be left to others less sensitive than himself. Then, next morning, he's faced with particular problems to be solved, and he just gets up without more ado, like a labourer starting a day's work.

The old woman winding wool by the fireplace is the Nurse who brought up the two girls, and the elderly lady beside her, busy with her knitting, is Eurydice, Creon's wife. She'll go on knitting right through the tragedy, until it's her turn to stand up and die. She is kind, dignified, loving. She is of no help to Creon. He is alone. Alone with his little page who is too small and can't be of any help to him either.

II

The pale youth alone on the other side of the room, leaning pensively against the wall, is the Messenger. He's the one who will in due course come and tell of Haemon's death. That's why he doesn't feel like talking and laughing with the others. He knows . . .

Lastly, those three red-faced fellows playing cards, with their caps pushed back on their heads – they're the guards. Not bad chaps. They've got wives . . . children . . . little worries the same as everyone else. But before long they'll be collaring the accused without turning a hair. They smell of garlic and leather and red wine, and are completely devoid of imagination. They are the agents – eternally complacent – of justice. For the time being the justice they serve is the justice of Creon . . . until the day comes when Thebes designates Creon's successor, and they are ordered to arrest Creon himself.

And now that you know them all they can act out their story.

Translation by Barbara Bray

COMMENTARY: Anouilh's modern version of *Antigone* was a conscious attempt to cloak in myth the dilemma facing the French people during the World War II occupation by the Nazis. By camouflaging his ideas behind a well-known classical tale, the dramatist was able to explore freely the moral ambiguity posed by collaboration with the enemy. In his play Antigone prefers to die rather than compromise her integrity in a morally corrupt world. Today the play is frequently revived. The conflict and debate between Antigone and Creon have lost none of their impact or relevance. As with all Anouilh's plays it provides actors with well-crafted roles and eminently speakable dialogue that forces the audience to listen.

The Prologue's speech has none of the cadences of an ancient Greek tragedy. It is written in familiar, colloquial language. The typical Greek Chorus of twelve performers is here reduced to a single person. He is an elegant man about town, drawing us into the tragedy with smooth talk, pointing to the play's main protagonists and antagonists as if they were guests at a cocktail party. He is a cool and detached observer, keen to have us know but emotionally uninvolved. His speech is arch and ironic. He is elaborating on background details for those in the audience who may not know the Antigone myth. He takes the audience into his confidence and steps beyond the fourth wall to address them directly. The challenge here for the actor is to balance the presentation of gossipy character sketches with the necessary historical background and details. Think about the rapport you can develop with your listeners as you perform this speech. It is up to you to deliver information clearly and maintain their interest in your story. Since you are invisible to the other characters, you can move about the stage with each paragraph to get different perspectives on the speech. You must tantalize the audience with your narrative, luring them into the web of tragic consequences.

Becket
(1959) Jean Anouilh

Act 3. Becket's cell.

Thomas à Becket (30s) is the Archbishop of Canterbury. Before his elevation to this position he was the bosom friend of King Henry II; together they shared a passion for women, hunting and the good life. Henry first appointed Becket as Chancellor of England and then made him Archbishop as a political move against the Church. Becket accepted the appointments although he argued that the second would destroy his close friendship with the King. The two men come into increasing conflict as Becket defends the Church against Henry's attempted incursions. The loyalty he displayed as a friend he now devotes solely to God. He abandons his luxurious lifestyle in favour of a rigorous spirituality. Eventually Becket is forced to flee England, finding protection under the French king. He then goes to Rome to seek Papal authority for his stand against Henry. In this monologue he reflects on his dilemma.

BECKET. Yet it would be simple enough. Too simple perhaps. Saintliness is a temptation too. Oh, how difficult it is to get an answer from You, Lord! I was slow in praying to You, but I cannot believe that others, worthier than I, who have spent years asking You questions, have been better than myself at deciphering Your real intentions. I am only a beginner and I must make mistake after mistake, as I did in my Latin translations as a boy, when my riotous imagination made the old priest roar with laughter. But I cannot believe that one learns Your language as one learns any human tongue, by hard studying, with a dictionary, a grammar and a set of idioms. I am sure that to the hardened sinner, who drops to his knees for the first time and murmurs Your name, marvelling, You tell him all Your secrets, straightaway, and that he understands. I have served You like a dilettante, surprised that I could still find my pleasure in Your service. And for a long time I was on my guard because of it. I could not believe this pleasure would bring me one step nearer You. I could not believe that the road could be a happy one. Their hair shirts, their fasting, their bells in the small hours summoning one to meet You, on the icy paving stones, in the sick misery of the poor ill-treated human animal – I cannot believe that all these are anything but safeguards for the weak. In power and in luxury, and even in the pleasures of the flesh, I shall not cease to speak to You, I feel this now. You are the God of the rich man and the happy man too, Lord and therein lies Your profound justice. You do not turn away Your eyes from the man who was given everything from birth. You have not abandoned him, alone in his ensnaring facility. And he may be Your true lost sheep. For Your scheme of things, which we mistakenly call Justice, is secret and profound and You plumb the hidden depths of poor men's puny frames as carefully as those of Kings. And beneath those outward differences, which blind us, but which to You are barely noticeable; beneath the diadem or the grime, You discern the same pride, the same vanity, the same petty, complacent preoccupation with oneself. Lord, I am certain now that You meant to tempt me with this hair shirt, object of so much vapid self-congratulation! this bare cell, this solitude, this absurdly endured winter-cold – and the conveniences of prayer. It would be too easy to buy You like this, at so low a price. I shall leave this convent, where so many precautions hem You round. I shall take up the mitre and the golden cope again, and the great silver cross, and I shall go back and fight in the place and with the weapons it has pleased You to give me. It has pleased You to make me Archbishop and to set me, like a solitary pawn, face to face with the King, upon the chess-board. I shall go back to my place, humbly, and let the world accuse me of pride, so that I may do what I believe is my life's work. For the rest, Your will be done. (*He crosses himself.*)

Translation by Lucienne Hill

COMMENTARY: Anouilh's *Becket* portrays the evolution of a saintly martyr. Anouilh created the character of King Henry II as the perfect foil to Becket. The shifting relationship between these two men, as friends and then enemies, is at the centre of the drama. Their characters are perfectly matched for conflict and two lead actors usually play these equally weighted but contrasting roles. Anouilh portrays Becket as a spiritual romantic, unsullied by pragmatic concerns, and Henry as a headstrong sensualist, who will not be contradicted. Becket is a demanding role that challenges the actor to transform from impetuous rake to saint. Anouilh's political rogue turned saintly martyr has attracted actors as various as Laurence Olivier, Richard Burton (film version) and Derek Jacobi. (*Compare Anouilh's version with T. S. Eliot's view of the same character on page* 97.)

What distinguishes this speech is its unadorned simplicity. Becket is speaking directly with his God, openly but privately in conversation. The repeated words 'You' and 'Your' are reverently stressed. He dwells on the dangers of saintliness, and how easy it is to confuse it with pride (a sin). At this point in the play Becket has forsaken his earthly comrade, King Henry, and a life of pleasure for intimate communion with a heavenly Lord and a life of transcendence. Yet, as Becket says, he's still a novice who is just learning how to take on a whole new role ('only a beginner'). Throughout the monologue Becket is attempting to strip away layers of human conceit to reveal the essential man. Each of his long speeches in the play is a step in this direction. Notice how the word 'shall' repeats itself like a litany. Becket's speech is like a prayer directed upwards. The actor always must remember that the character is not purely a holy man but also a former soldier. He is a unique combination of flesh and spirit. There is nothing blind about him; he goes towards his fate with his eyes open. The speech keeps both sides of the character on view and in tension. This is probably Becket's most open and vulnerable moment in the play. At this point the stage becomes his confessional and the audience is in the intimate position of hearing his private thoughts.

Bingo

(1973) Edward Bond

Scene 4. A room in the Golden Cross Inn. Warwickshire, 1615.

Ben Jonson (30s) comes to visit the ageing Shakespeare to find out if he has a new play under way. Shakespeare has been both a rival and a mentor to the younger Jonson. Compared to the taciturn Shakespeare, Jonson is garrulous and talkative. During his two-hour wait for Shakespeare he has been drinking heavily. Now both men are drinking together and begin to quarrel about money and art. As he reveals in this speech, Jonson is a blunt, volatile, passionate and jealous man.

JONSON. Patronizing bastard. (*Slight pause. They drink.*) You don't want to quarrel with me. I killed one once. Fellow writer. Only way to end a literary quarrel. Put my sword in him. Like a new pen. The blood flowed as if inspired. Then the Old Bailey. I was going to hang. That's carrying research too far. I could read so they let me off. Proper respect for learning. Branded my thumb. A child's alphabet: 'T' for Tyburn. I've been in prison four times. Dark smelly places. No gardens. Sorry yours is too big. They kept coming in and taking people out to cut bits off them. Their hands. Take off their noses. Cut their stomachs open. Rummage round inside with a dirty fist and drag everything out. The law. Little men going out through the door. White. Shaking. Even staggering. I ask, is it necessary? What's your life been like? Any real blood, any prison? Four times? Don't go, don't go. I want to touch you for a loan. I know I'm not human. My father died before I was born. That desperate to avoid me. My eyes are too close together. Look. A well

18

known fact. I used to have so much good will when I was young. That what's necessary, isn't it? Good will. In the end. O god. (*Silence. They drink.*) Yes. (*Silence.*) What are you writing?

[SHAKESPEARE. I think you're a very good writer. I made them put on your first play.]

God, am I that bad? In prison they threatened to cut off my nose. And ears. They didn't offer to work on my eyes. Life doesn't seem to touch you, I mean soil you. You walk by on the clean pavement. I climb tall towers to show I'm clever. Others do tricks in the gutter. You are serene. Serene. I'm going to make you drunk and watch you spew. You aren't weii, I can see that! Something's happening to your will. You're being sapped. I think you're dying. What a laugh! Are you getting hollow? Why don't you get up? Walk out? Why are you listening to my hysterical crap? Don't worry about me. I'll survive. I've lived through two religious conversions. I thrive on tearing myself to bits. I even bought enough poison. Once. In a moment of strength. (*He takes a small bottle from his collar. It hangs round his neck on a chain.*) I was too weak to take it. Hung the cross here in my catholic period. (*He takes the top off the bottle.*) Look: coated in sugar. Like to lick my poison? I licked one once to try. (SHAKE-SPEARE *doesn't react.*) Well, it's not the best. All I could afford. Little corner shop in London.

[SHAKESPEARE. Give it to me.]

Sentimental whiner. You wouldn't uncross your legs if I ate the lot. You're upset I might give it to someone else. (*He puts the bottle back in his collar.*) I should live in the country. No – I'd hear myself talk. When I went sight-seeing in the mad house there was a young man who spent all his time stamping on his shadow. Punched it. Went for it with a knife. Tried to cut the head off. Anything to be free. The knife on the stone. The noise. Sparks. (*They drink.*) I helped to uncover the gunpowder plot. Keep in with the top. (*They*

19

drink.) Your health. I'm always saying nice things about you, Serenity. Of course, I touch on your lack of education, or as I put it genuine ignorance. But you can't ignore an elephant when it waves at you with its trunk, can you. You taking this down? Base something on me. A minor character who comes on for five minutes while the lead's off changing his clothes or making a last effort to learn his lines? Shall I tell you something about me? I hate. Yes – isn't that interesting! I keep it well hidden but it's true: I hate. A short hard word. Begins with a hiss and ends with a spit: hate. To say it you open your mouth as if you're bringing up: hate. I hate you, for example. For preference actually. Hate's far more jealous than love. You can't satisfy it by the gut or the groin. A terrible appetite. Interrupt me. Speak. Sob. Nothing? I'm not afraid to let myself be insulted. . . . Where was I? Yes: hate. I hate you because you smile. Right up to *under* your eyes. Which are set the right distance apart. O I've wiped the smile off now. I hate your health. I'm sure you'll die in a healthy way. Well at least you're dying. That's incense to scatter on these burning coals. I hate your long country limbs. I've seen you walking along the city streets like a man going over his own fields. So simple. A simple stride. So beautiful and simple. You see why I hate you. How have they made you so simple? Tell me, Will? Please. How have they made you so good? You even know when it's time to die. Come down here to die quietly in your garden or an upstairs room. My death will be terrible. I'll linger on in people's way, poor, thick, dirty, empty, a mess. I go on and on, why can't I stop? I even talk shit now. To know the seasons of life and death and walk quietly on the path between them. No tears, no tears. Hate is like a clown armed with a knife. He must draw blood to cap the joke, you know? Well, have you got a new play, it has to be a comedy, rebuilding is expensive, they'd like you to invest. Think about it. You may come up with an idea, or manage to steal one. But it must be in time for next season. (*Silence*.) My life's been one long self-insult. It came on with puberty. (*Silence*. JONSON *drinks*.) Teach me something.

COMMENTARY: Bond's *Bingo*, a stark historical play that sounds so modern, sets out to demystify artistic greatness by placing it squarely in a cruel and violent social context. Bond presents William Shakespeare and Ben Jonson first and foremost as tough, pragmatic men and only secondly as authors of genius. By knocking the characters off their high literary pedestals and bringing them down to earth, Bond reveals them as flawed individuals, liberating them for the performer. This Ben Jonson has to be *your* version of the man and not the man transmitted to us by history.

Bond's Jonson is bluff and profane. Look at his sardonic opening line. He is cruel, ironic and self-deprecating. His relationship to Shakespeare is based on rivalry and, most importantly, jealousy. Notice that he speaks in short, sharp, declarative sentences, often using just two or three words to convey a thought. Sometimes just one word is sufficient to express his venom. He uses simple monosyllabic nouns and verbs to solid effect ('A short hard word'). There is nothing even slightly florid and literary about his language yet the bluff talk is oddly poetic. Words are used like building stones, reminding us that the real Ben Jonson was a one-time bricklayer. He's like some latter-day working-class poet. The character's life has been one of close escapes from the gallows ('Tyburn' was London's hanging fields). It's all left him with a self-lacerating wit ('I thrive on tearing myself to bits.') and a tattoo on his thumb. The Jonson we get here is a man of experience and not just pure imagination (that's Shakespeare's role). To Jonson everything is as plain as the nose on your face. A sword and a pen are interchangeable. The speech is full of startling images: from the prop of poison around his neck to the 'young man who spent all his time stamping on his shadow'. Jonson is full of mad energy and brawling anger. Each time the word 'hate' is uttered it should strike the audience like a red-hot poker. Hate also reveals a deep streak of disillusionment in Jonson. Here's a man who has lost his good will sitting and talking to someone whose good will is boundless. Notice that he is in awe of Shakespeare which is where the conflict for the character lies. This is a long speech divided into three parts. The actor must be able to sustain it over a concentrated period of time, following Jonson's rambling rant to its drunken and pathetic conclusion.

The Blood Knot
(1961) Athol Fugard

Scene 3. A one-room shack in the non-White slum area of Korsten near Port Elizabeth, South Africa. Evening.

Zachariah (40s) is a dark-skinned South African. He has a light-skinned brother, Morris (see following monologue), who often passes as white in a segregated society. Although they were born to the same Coloured (mixed-race) mother they had different fathers. Zach works as a security guard and is uneducated and illiterate. After many years away, pursuing his education and an independent life, Morris unexpectedly returns to live with his brother. They spend their time talking and reminiscing about the past. They dream of a better future with a small farm of their own. More than anything Zach desires a 'woman'. Morris encourages him to find a female pen-pal, and even starts writing letters for him to eighteen-year-old Ethel. When Morris sees from a photo that Ethel is white, he realizes that Zach has no intention of telling her that he is Coloured. Under South Africa's stringent apartheid laws, inter-racial sex is a crime and Morris knows that Zach's fantasy presents a dangerous threat. Morris demands that he burn her letters and photo, Zach responds with this speech.

ZACHARIAH. Wait . . . wait . . . wait . . . not so fast. I'm a sort of slow man. We were talking about this letter, not her. Now tell me, what's wrong with what you did read? Does she call me names? No. Does she laugh at me? No. Does she swear at me? No. Just a simple letter with a little bit of this and a little bit of that. Now comes the clue. What sort of chap is it that throws away a few kind words? Hey, Morrie? Aren't they, as you say, precious things these days? And this pretty picture of a lovely girl? I burn it! What sort of doing is that? Bad. Think of Ethel, man. Think! Sitting

23

up there in Oudtshoorn with Lucy, waiting . . . waiting . . . for what? For nothing. For why? Because bad Zach Pietersen burnt it. No, Morrie. Good is good, fair is fair, and I may be a shade of black, but I go gently as a man.

[MORRIS. Are you finished? (*Pause.*) I just want to remind you, Zach, that when I was writing to her you weren't even interested in a single thing I said. *Ja* . . . *Ja* . . . Okay . . . Okay. . . . That's all that came from you. But now, suddenly, now you are! Why? Why, I ask myself . . . and a suspicious little voice answers: Is it maybe because she's white? (*Pause.*) Well?]

Okay. Do you want to hear me say it? (MORRIS *says nothing.*) It's because she's white! I like this little white girl! I like the thought of this little white girl. I'm thinking it, now. Look at me. *Ja.* Can't you see? I'm serious, but I'm also smiling. I'm telling you I like the thought of this little white Ethel better than our future, or the plans, or getting away, or foot-salts, or any other damned thing in here. It's a warm thought for a man in winter. It's the best thought I ever had and I'm keeping it. So maybe it's a error as you say. Well, that's just too bad. We done it, and now I got it and I'm keeping it, and don't you try no tricks like trying to get it away from me. Who knows? You might get to liking it too. (MORRIS *says nothing.* ZACHARIAH *comes closer.*) *Ja.* There's a thought there. What about *you*, Morrie? You never had it before? . . . that thought? A man like you, specially you, always thinking so many things? A man like you who's been places! You're always telling me about the places you been. Wasn't there ever no white woman thereabouts? I mean. . . . You must have smelt them someplace. That sweet, white smell, you know. They leave it behind. (*Nudging* MORRIS.) Of course you did. Hey? I bet you had that thought all the time. I bet you been having it in here. Hey? You should have shared it, Morrie. I'm a man with a taste for thoughts these days. It hurts to think you didn't

24

share a good one like that with your brother. Giving me all that shit about future and plans, and then keeping the real goosie for yourself. You weren't scared, were you? That I would tell? Come on. Confess. You were scared, hey! A little bit poopy. I've noticed that. But you needn't worry now. I'm a man for keeping a secret, and anyway, we'll play this very careful . . . very, very careful. Ethel won't never know about us, and I know how to handle that brother. Mustn't let a policeman bugger you about, man. So go get your pencil and piece of paper. (MORRIS *defeated. He sits at the table.* ZACHARIAH *paces.*) We'll go gently with this one. There'll be others . . . later. So we'll take her on friendly terms again. (*Pause.*) 'Dear Ethel, . . . (MORRIS *writes.*) I think you might like to know I got your letter, and the picture. I'd say Oudtshoorn seems all right. You were quite all right too. I would like to send you a picture of me, but it's this way. It's winter down here now. The light is bad, the lake is black, the birds have gone. Wait for spring, when things improve. Okay? Good. I heard you ask about my car. Yes. I have it. We pumped the tyres today. Tomorrow I think I'll put in some petrol. I'd like to take you for a drive, Ethel, and Lucy too. In fact, I'd like to drive both of you. They say over here, I'm fast. I'll tell you this. If I could drive you, I would do it so fast, Ethel, and Lucy too, both of you, so fast I would, it would hurt . . .'

COMMENTARY: Athol Fugard's *The Blood Knot* is the story of Zach and Morris; two brothers fatally shackled by the ties of blood. The play explores the specific pain and degradation caused by apartheid set against the harsh cruelties of everyday life and family relations. The racial turmoil that has gripped South Africa and made it a divided country is just one of many factors in the lives of Fugard's tormented characters. Unlike most overtly political modern drama, however, Athol Fugard's plays work because of their deep humanity and emotional intensity. His dramas are always about people first and foremost.

Although deep racial segregation and prejudice form the background to Fugard's *The Blood Knot*, this speech uncovers the deep sibling rivalry between two brothers that gives the drama its immediacy. That conflict puts all the grander, ideological tensions into sharper relief. Zach is out to prove he is the better man, a gentler man than his brother Morris. In the world of this play a white woman is like a prize gardenia: fragrant and exotic. The image of Ethel, though no physical description of her is provided in this speech, is enough to conjure up both a liberating vision and a threatening barrier. Writing letters to her is a challenge. Notice, too, that this speech gives Zach a chance to revolt against Morris's intellectual superiority. Zach displays the ability to 'think' for himself, to take control of the scene. The actor should never lose sight of the fact that this is partly a humorous speech (many letter-writing speeches are) and that comic moments come in the later dictation parts where Zach records the mundane act of taking the women for a ride. Morris's implied reaction to this dictation must also be kept in focus by the performer. Morris is trying to impress his brother as much as Ethel.

Scene 4. The following evening.

In the next scene Zach receives another letter from Ethel which Morris reads to him. She writes of her plan to come and visit him. As Zach confronts his dilemma, Morris tries to persuade him to reveal the truth about 'the colour of his skin' to Ethel.

MORRIS. Then tell me what else you can say. Come on. Let's hear it. What is there a man can say or pray that will change the colour of his skin or blind them to it?
[ZACHARIAH. There must be something.]
I'm telling you there's nothing. When it's a question of

smiles, and whispers, and thoughts in strange eyes . . . there is only the truth and. . . . (*He pauses.*)

[ZACHARIAH. And what then?]

And then to make a run for it. Yes. They don't like these games with their whiteness. You've heard them. 'How would you like your daughter to correspond with a black man?' Ethel's got a policeman brother and an uncle and *your* address.

[ZACHARIAH. What have I done, hey? I done nothing.]

What have you thought? That's the question. That's the crime. I seem to remember somebody saying: 'I like the thought of this little white girl.' And what about your dreams? They've kept me awake these past few nights, Zach. I've heard them, mumbling and moaning away in the darkness. They'll hear them quick enough. When they get their hands on a dark-born boy playing with a white idea, you think they don't find out what he's been dreaming at night? They have ways and means, my friend. Mean ways. Like confinement, in a cell, on bread and water, for days without end. They sit outside with their ears to the keyhole and wait . . . and wait. They got time. You'll get tired. So they wait. And soon you do, and no matter how you fight, your eyeballs start rolling round and . . . around and then, before you know it, maybe while you're still praying, before you can cry, or scream for help . . . you fall asleep and dream! All they need for evidence is a man's dreams. Not so much his hate. They say they can live with that. It's his dreams they drag off to judgment shouting: 'Silence! He's been caught! With convictions? He's pleading! He's guilty! Take him away.' (*Pause.*) Where? You ask where with your eyes, I see. You know where, Zach. You've seen them, in the streets, carrying their spades and the man with his gun. Bald heads, short trousers, and that ugly jersey with the red, painful red stripes around the body. (MORRIS *goes back to the window.*) I miss the moths. They made the night a friendly sort of place. (*Turning to* ZACHARIAH.) What are you going to do about it, Zach?

COMMENTARY: Unlike his dark-skinned brother (*see previous monologue and introduction*), Morris is light-skinned and so has one foot firmly in the white world. This fact of life makes him keenly aware of the dangers of racial mixing. It is in his blood and genes, so to speak, to sound warning bells. Morris tries to frighten his brother with his descriptions of 'them' and what 'they' will do to Zach. The speech is resigned to the bitter realities and ugliness of apartheid and racial separation. The actor doing this speech must decide, too, whether or not Morris is trying to exclude his black brother from a world that Morris safely but secretly inhabits. So much of this play is about the jealousy and rivalry between half-brothers. In the world of this drama, 'thinking' about whites seems to be as much of a crime as mingling with them. That, at least, is a notion that Morris is reinforcing. The speech is written like one of those hazardous warning labels you find on toxic substances. Morris is well spoken and articulate; his powers of persuasion must come through in performance. The influence he exerts over the less articulate Zach is achieved mainly through his superior command of language. He ends his speech with a challenging question.

Blues for Mister Charlie
(1964) James Baldwin

Act 1. Papa D's Juke Joint. An unnamed town in the deep South.

Richard Henry (20s), after eight years as a singer in New York (at the Apollo Theatre in Harlem), returns to his home town to recover from drug abuse and rebuild his life. His father, a respected black preacher, supports non-violence and tries to improve relations between the black and white communities. Richard blames his father for not avenging the death of his mother. In this scene he speaks to Juanita, his former girlfriend, who has plans to go up north to law school, boasting of the 'white chicks' he seduced in New York, showing her pictures of his conquests. Juanita keeps asking him about how 'sick' he was and he finally answers her with this speech.

RICHARD. I was a junkie. . . . A junkie, a dope addict, a hophead, a mainliner – a dope fiend! My arms and my legs, too, are full of holes! . . . I got hooked about five years ago. See, I couldn't stand these chicks I was making it with, and I was working real hard at my music, and man, I was lonely. You come off a gig, you be tired, and you'd already taken as much shit as you could stand from the managers and the people in the room you were working and you'd be off to make some down scene with some pasty white-faced bitch. And so you'd make the scene and somehow you'd wake up in the morning and the chick would be beside you, alive and well, and dying to make the scene again and somehow you'd manage not to strangle her, you hadn't beaten her to death. Like you wanted to. And you get out of there and you carry this pain around inside all day and all night long. No way to beat it – no *way*. No matter how you turned, no matter what

29

you did – no *way*. But when I started getting high, I was cool, and it didn't bother me. And I wasn't lonely then, it was all right. And the chicks – I could handle them, they couldn't reach me. And I didn't know I was hooked – until I was *hooked*. Then I started getting into trouble and I lost a lot of gigs and I had to sell my car and I lost my pad and most of the chicks, they split, naturally – but not all of them – and then I got busted and I made that trip down to Lexington and – here I am. Way *down* upon the Swanee River. But I'm going to be all right. You can bet on it.

COMMENTARY: James Baldwin's *Blues for Mister Charlie* revolves around a racial murder. It evokes a time and place in America when the tension between whites and blacks was at its fiercest. During the 1960s Baldwin's writing became synonymous with the struggle for black rights and the declaration of a black voice in drama. Like so many modern American plays it is about a journey and about outsiders. *Blues for Mister Charlie* is one of Baldwin's most lyrical creations, revealing a great humanity and an uncompromising honesty. If you compare his writing with that of, say, Athol Fugard (*see the two previous monologues*) you'll notice a close kinship. Their characters are representative of an underclass; individuals caught in the crossfire of hatred and racial mixing.

Richard is a man of passion and charisma. He finally gives way to Juanita's repeated questions and launches into this temperamental, teeming confession. Remember that Richard is a singer/musician. Notice the bluesy musicality of Richard's words and phrasing, reflecting the 'blues' in the title of the play. There is a deep rage and pain at the heart of this speech, being black and being a drug addict are intertwined. Suppressing the urge for drugs and for rage lie at the heart of the speech. Notice how rapidly Richard speaks. It is as if his years of drug addiction have altered his metabolism. The sentences are figuratively strung out. Richard is hemmed in by his words; they push him into a corner. The narrative becomes a sorry tale about losing control, losing self-respect. Think of the speech as a journey. Richard is telling

Juanita just how he got from there to here, from up North to down South, from fame to failure. This is an admission of failure, a tale of the blues and a reaching out to someone for relief.

Act 3. Parnell's bedroom. Night.

Parnell James (30s–40s) is the white editor of the local newspaper. He is a wealthy and sophisticated southern gentleman with a strong liberal streak and is a fervent supporter of black rights. For years he has been attracted to various black women including Juanita. Richard Henry (see monologue above) is murdered after he picks a quarrel with Lyle, a bigoted local shopkeeper, who also happens to be Parnell's oldest friend. In the preceding scene Lyle's trial for murder is underway and Parnell has just been called. This monologue immediately follows as a character flashback. Parnell, in his dressing-gown after attempting to make love to an unnamed white woman, confronts his real passions.

PARNELL. She says I called somebody else's name. What name could I have called? And she won't repeat the name. Well. That's enough to freeze the blood and arrest the holy, the liberating orgasm! Christ, how weary I am of this dull calisthenic called love – with no love in it! What name could I have called? I hope it was – a *white* girl's name, anyway! Ha-ha! How still she became! And I hardly realized it, I was too far away – and then it was too late. And she was just looking at me. Jesus! To have somebody just looking at you – just looking at you – like that – at such a moment! It makes you feel – like you woke up and found yourself in bed with your mother! I tried to find out what was wrong – poor girl! But there's nothing you can say at a moment like that – really nothing. You're caught. Well, haven't I kept telling her that there's no future for her with me? There's no future for me with anybody! But that's all right. What name could I have

31

called? I haven't been with anybody else for a long time, a long time. She said I haven't been with her, either. I guess she's right. I've just been using her. Using her as an anchor – to hold me here, in this house, this bed – so I won't find myself on the other side of town, ruining my reputation. *What* reputation? They all know. I swear they all *know*. Know what? What's there to know? So you get drunk and you fool around a little. Come on, Parnell. There's more to it than that. That's the reason you draw blanks whenever you get drunk. Everything comes out. Everything. They see what you don't dare to see. What name could I have called? Richard would say that you've got – black fever! Yeah, and he'd be wrong – that long, loud, black mother. I wonder if she's asleep yet – or just lying there, looking at the walls. Poor girl! All your life you've been made sick, stunned, dizzy, oh Lord! driven half mad by blackness. Blackness in front of your eyes. Boys and girls, men and women – you've bowed down in front of them all! And then hated yourself. Hated yourself for debasing yourself? Out with it, Parnell! The nigger-lover! Black boys and girls! I've wanted my hands full of them, wanted to drown them, laughing and dancing and making love – making love – wow! – and be transformed, formed, liberated out of this grey-white envelope. Jesus! I've always been afraid. Afraid of what I saw in their eyes! They don't love me, certainly. You don't love them, either! Sick with a disease only white men catch. Blackness. What is it like to be black? To look out on the world from *that* place? I give nothing! How dare she say that! My girl, if you knew what I've given! Ah. Come off it, Parnell. To *whom* have you given? What name did I call? What name did I call?

COMMENTARY: The scene of this speech is significant. It is a bedroom; a place of sanctuary, privacy, dreams and amorous

meetings. All of these notions come into play during the monologue. Parnell is a divided and guilty man: a southern white liberal
with a black mistress who must function in a white supremacist
society. He is accepted and equally respected by both white and
black worlds. His role in this play is a pivotal one since he is a close
friend of the white bigot who kills a young black man. His loyalty
and integrity are divided and tested. A confusion of racial
allegiance is brought to a head in this speech. Conscience and
libido are curiously intertwined to show how passion and reason
unsettle one another, leaving Parnell disoriented. Parnell's
thought process is as confusing and orgasmic as the sexual act. The
speech is somewhat abstract and is meant to capture the feel of a
late night reverie. There is an unmistakable musicality to the
speech that helps to underscore Parnell's despair.

Caligula
(1945) Albert Camus

Act 3. A room in the Imperial Palace, Rome.

Caligula (20s) is the young, handsome Emperor of Rome. His extreme grief, following the death three years ago of Drusilla, his sister and his incestuous mistress, has shattered his faith in a benign universe. His statement that 'men die and are not happy' encapsulates his new grim viewpoint. With unlimited power at his disposal he embarks on an indiscriminate campaign of torture, blasphemy and murder to rival the cruelty of the gods. He abandons the demands of traditional logic, morality, and humanity and challenges the accepted limitations of the physical world. One of his schemes is to bring the moon to earth with the help of his only remaining friend and supporter, Helicon. In this speech he contemplates his isolation.

CALIGULA *(falls to pacing the room. After a while he approaches the mirror).* You decided to be logical, didn't you, poor simpleton? Logic for ever! The question now is: Where will that take you? *(Ironically.)* Suppose the moon were brought here, everything would be different. That was the idea, wasn't it? Then the impossible would become possible, in a flash the Great Change come, and all things be transfigured. After all, why shouldn't Helicon bring it off? One night, perhaps, he'll catch her sleeping in a lake, and carry her here, trapped in a glistening net, all slimy with weeds and water, like a pale bloated fish drawn from the depths. Why not, Caligula? Why not, indeed? *(He casts a glance round the room.)* Fewer and fewer people round me; I wonder why. *(Addressing the mirror in a muffled voice.)* Too many dead, too many dead – that makes an emptiness. . . .

No, even if the moon were mine, I could not retrace my way. Even were those dead men thrilling again under the sun's caress, the murders wouldn't go back underground for that. (*Angrily.*) Logic, Caligula; follow where logic leads. Power to the uttermost; wilfulness without end. Ah, I'm the only man on earth to know the secret – that power can never be complete without a total self-surrender to the dark impulse of one's destiny. No, there's no return. I must go on and on, until the consummation.

Translation by Stuart Gilbert

COMMENTARY: Camus' *Caligula* examines the absurd and irrational nature of human existence. In the play Caligula continually confronts his realization that the world has become meaningless; he is a negative idealist. He does not oppose absurdity with intellectual debate; he believes his only option is passionate, direct action. There is no alternative, no moral middle ground. In his personal revolt everything is arbitrary and cruel. Caligula is similar to a character in one of Camus' later works who states, 'I revolt, therefore we are'. Camus' famous philosophy of the 'outsider', so cogently illustrated in his seminal modern novel *L'Etranger*, receives a more graphic treatment in his portrait of Caligula, that most brutal and depraved of ancient Rome's emperors.

Caligula's self-absorption is boldly realized in this monologue to himself in a mirror. Narcissism is part of the young emperor's nature. This speech is literally a self-encounter. The logic of choice and free will – which, when set in motion, can easily be taken to extreme ends – is the subject of the speech. By bending the rules of logic, blinding himself to morality and trusting in his own self-imposed image of power, Caligula becomes the kind of dictator all subsequent dictators have used as their model: an autocrat ruled only by himself. What we are exposed to is an extraordinary mind warped by tricks of thinking and a personal code of justice. The art for the actor is to make this repellent habit of mind appear attractive. Caligula uses words to convince himself. Phrases like, 'Logic, Caligula; follow where logic leads. Power to the uttermost;

wilfulness without end,' become standards to live and act by. Notice the elevation and eloquence of Caligula's diction. What the actor is revealing is a mind in the grips of obsessive delusion and paranoia. Yet Caligula is no fool. He recognizes the absurd and revolts against it.

The Caretaker

(1960) Harold Pinter

Act 2. A cluttered room in a house in West London filled with junk and broken-down furniture.

Mick (late 20s) is Aston's younger brother. Aston lives in a room which he offers to share with Davies, a shabby, old tramp. Davies has to get to Sidcup to replace his lost documentation and 'papers', but he cannot do so until he acquires a pair of shoes. Once in the room Davies finds all manner of excuses to get out of leaving. While Aston is out, Mick arrives and finds Davies going through his brother's belongings. He attacks and intimidates him. Mick changes tactic as the second act begins, treating Davies with a combination of exaggerated respect and violent contempt. In this speech Mick once again turns on Davies.

MICK. You're stinking the place out. You're an old robber, there's no getting away from it. You're an old skate. You don't belong in a nice place like this. You're an old barbarian. Honest. You got no business wandering about in an unfurnished flat. I could charge seven quid a week for this if I wanted to. Get a taker tomorrow. Three hundred and fifty a year exclusive. No argument. I mean, if that sort of money's in your range don't be afraid to say so. Here you are. Furniture and fittings, I'll take four hundred or the nearest offer. Rateable value ninety quid for the annum. You can reckon water, heating and lighting at close on fifty. That'll cost you eight hundred and ninety if you're all that keen. Say the word and I'll have my solicitors draft you out a contract. Otherwise I've got the van outside, I can run you to the police station in five minutes, have you in for trespassing, loitering with intent, daylight robbery, filching, thieving and stinking the place out. What do you say? Unless you're really keen on a straightforward purchase. Of course, I'll get my brother to decorate it up for you first. I've got a brother who's a number one decorator. He'll decorate it up for you. If you want more space, there's four more rooms along the landing ready to go. Bathroom, living-room, bedroom and nursery. You can have this as your study. This brother I mentioned, he's just about to start on the other rooms. Yes, just about to start. So what do you say? Eight hundred odd for this room or three thousand down for the whole upper storey. On the other hand, if you prefer to approach it in the long-term way I know an insurance firm in West Ham'll be pleased to handle the deal for you. No strings attached, open and above board, untarnished record; twenty per cent interest, fifty per cent deposit; down payments, back payments, family allowances, bonus schemes, remission of term for good behaviour, six months lease, yearly examination of the relevant archives, tea laid on, disposal of shares, benefit extension, compensation on cessation, comprehensive indemnity against Riot, Civil Commotion, Labour Disturbances, Storm, Tempest, Thunderbolt, Larceny or Cattle all subject to a daily check and double check. Of course we'd need a signed declaration from your personal medical attendant as assurance that you possess the requisite fitness to carry the can, won't we? Who do you bank with? (*Pause.*) Who do you bank with?

COMMENTARY: Pinter's *The Caretaker* is justly celebrated as a high-voltage comedy of menace. It is one of the modern theatre's most durable and dangerous dramas, having a strong influence on such well-known contemporary plays as David Mamet's *American Buffalo* (*see page* 7) and Lyle Kessler's *Orphans*. At the root of every scene is a deadly territorial struggle for power and survival.

This particular speech walks a very fine line between the comic and the serious. It cries out for bravura acting. Notice what a chameleon Mick is when it comes to words and ideas. He can change shape and persona as he speaks, shifting from one idiom to another. Mick's fiery, foul attack on Davies ('You're stinking the place out') suddenly shifts from being a high pressure sales pitch to a threatening rant. Mick is offering Davies a good deal that he is willing to put in the form of a contract. Look at the elaborate way Mick sets out all the terms in a breathless stream of clauses and addendum. He never allows Davies the chance to get a word in edgeways but strong-arms him into a choice that seems to settle the matter. Mick simply overpowers him with the force of his delivery. Part of his strategy is to disorient Davies and surround him with a barrage of language. Thievery and robbery (both Mick and Davies are small time con-men) are two themes that the speech signals right from the start. The actor can use these images to help strike the right tone of Mick's aggressive arrogance. Think of Mick also as a character of amazing charm who chooses and uses words with great precision. All of his sentences are skilfully crafted and rhythmical. He speaks a form of street poetry. Mick is a 'barrow boy': a swift, sleight-of-hand, street trader with mesmerizing powers of persuasion who sweetens the offer with the illusion of added incentives. Throughout the play Mick, a shadowy loner, shows flashes of personality in solo speeches like this one. Yet much of what he says is pure bluff and display. He remains a character who is impossible to fathom and, at times, seems as afraid of the outside world as Davies.

The Caucasian Chalk Circle
(1948) Bertolt Brecht

Scene 5. Azdak's hut.

Azdak (30s) is the village scribe who prides himself on being an intellectual. He is a thief and a poacher. In a ragged and tipsy state he has returned to his shabby hut. He has offered refuge to a fugitive he found in a thicket. Azdak quickly discovers that his fugitive is not a beggar but a rich landowner on the run as a result of the raging civil war. They are interrupted by Shauva, the policeman, who has come to make Azdak hand over the 'rabbit'. When Azdak refuses Shauva asks him what action he should then take to retrieve one of the prince's 'rabbits'.

AZDAK. Shauva, Shauva, you ought to be ashamed. There you stand asking me a question when a question is the worst of all temptations. Suppose you were a woman, Nunovna, for instance, the wicked slut, and you show me the upper reaches of your leg, Nunovna's I mean, and ask me: What should I do about my leg, it itches – is she innocent, behaving like that? No. I catch rabbits, but you catch men. A man is made in God's image, a rabbit isn't, you know that. I'm a rabbit eater, but you're a cannibal, Shauva, and God will judge you. Go home, Shauva, and repent. No, wait a minute, maybe I've got something for you. (*He looks around at the fugitive who stands there trembling.*) No, never mind. Go home and repent. (*He slams the door in his face. To the fugitive.*) You're surprised, aren't you? That I didn't hand you over. But I couldn't even hand a bedbug over to that dumb-ox policeman, it goes against my grain. Never be afraid of a policeman. So old and such a coward. Eat up your cheese like a poor man, or they're sure to catch you. Do I have to show you how a poor man behaves? (*He pushes him down in his chair and puts the piece of cheese back in his hand*.) This chest is the table. Put your elbows on the table, surround the cheese on the plate as if it might be snatched away at any moment, can you ever be sure? Hold your knife like a small sickle and don't look at the cheese so greedily, your expression should be more on the sorrowful side, because it's already vanishing, like all beauty. (*Watches him*.) They're looking for you, that's in your favour, but how can I know they're not mistaken about you? In Tiflis one time they hanged a landowner, a Turk. He was able to prove that he didn't just cut his peasants in half the usual way, but quartered them. He gouged out twice as much taxes as anybody else, his zeal was above suspicion, but they hanged him as a criminal all the same, just because he was a Turk, which he couldn't help. That was an injustice. He found himself on the gallows the way Pontius Pilate found himself in the Creed. To make a long story short, I don't trust you.

Translation by Ralph Manheim

COMMENTARY: Brecht's *Caucasian Chalk Circle* uses a comic folk parable to dramatize a modern tale about survival, justice and salvation. Set in a war-torn landscape where human goodness seems doubtful the slightest gesture of kindness can become an extraordinary moral event. In this topsy-turvy world an unexpected twist in the plot sees the crooked Azdak appointed as a judge. He then subverts the legal system and a golden age of justice ensues. Brecht skilfully weaves three separate dramatic strands together which culminate in a trial overseen by the Solomon-like Azdak. The play concludes by implying that human nature, although not perfect, is certainly capable of improvement.

Azdak is a typical Brechtian hero: crafty, suspicious and pugnaciously comic. He can change guises and sides in the blink of an eye. Part of the challenge here for an actor is to show the many faces of this complex character who will never quite declare himself honestly. Is he a friend or foe, a comedian or a fiend? There is certainly a good deal of the con-man in Azdak and he delights in words and ideas, using them to perform verbal tricks. He also takes a malicious glee in tormenting his guest-cum-victim. Like a cat playing with a mouse, he looks the other way and then pounces on his prey. Azdak is also a downmarket philosopher who can see the absurdity of life and death. He is in no doubt that existence is perilous and that you've got to take care of yourself first. To Azdak no one can be trusted. He likes to hide behind homilies and aphorisms. In this speech he realizes and then relishes the power he has over a rich man, over law and authority. The last line is a wonderful climax to a very verbose speech.

Chips With Everything
(1962) Arnold Wesker

Act 2, scene 10. A roadway.

Smiler (18–20), a recent conscript in the RAF, runs away from training camp. He has been the target of scorn and harassment from superiors who 'have it in for him'. On the parade ground they interpret his easy smile as a sneer. The relentless drilling and abuse have finally made him crack. 'He is desperate, haggard and tired.' We find him on the motorway outside the camp, trying to hitch a ride.

SMILER. LEAVE ME ALONE! Damn your mouths and hell on your stripes – leave me alone. Mad they are, they're mad they are, they're raving lunatics they are. CUT IT! STUFF IT! Shoot your load on someone else, take it out on someone else, why do you want to pick on me, you lunatics, you bloody apes, you're nothing more than bloody apes, so damn your mouths and hell on your stripes! Ahhhhh – they'd kill me if they had the chance. They think they own you, think that anyone who's dressed in blue is theirs to muck about, degrade. YOU BLOODY APES, YOU WON'T DEGRADE ME! Oh my legs – I'm going home. I'll get a lift and scarper home. I'll go to France, I'll get away. I'LL GET AWAY FROM YOU, YOU APES! They think they own you – Oh my back. I don't give tuppence what you say, you don't mean anything to me, your bloody orders nor your stripes nor your jankers nor your wars. Stick your jankers on the wall, stuff yourselves, go away and stuff yourselves, stuff your rotten stupid selves – Ohh – Ohhh. Look at the sky, look at the moon, Jesus look at that moon

43

and the frost in the air. I'll wait. I'll get a lift in a second or two, it's quiet now, their noise is gone. I'll stand and wait and look at that moon. What are you made of, tell me? I don't know what you're made of, you go on and on. What grouses you? What makes you scream? You're blood and wind like all of us, what grouses you? You poor duff bastards, where are your mothers? Where were you born – I don't know what grouses you, your voices sound like dying hens – I don't know. That bloody lovely moon is cold, I can't stay here. I'll freeze to death. That's a laugh, now that'd fool them. Listen! A bike, a motor-bike, a roaring bloody motor-bike. (*Starts thumbing.*) London, London, London, London, LONDON! (*The roar comes and dies.*) You stupid ghet, I want a lift, can't you see I want a lift, an airman wants a lift back home. Home, you bastard, take me Ho'ooooome. (*Long pause.*) Now they'll catch me, now they'll come, not much point in going on – Smiler boy, they'll surely come, they're bound to miss you back at camp – eyes like hawks they've got – God! Who cares. 'Stop your silly smiling Airman' – 'It's not a smile, Corp, it's natural, honest, Corp. I'm born that way. Honest Corp, it's not a smile . . .'

COMMENTARY: In *Chips With Everything*, Arnold Wesker uses the military establishment to create a searing indictment of British society. The play illustrates the corruption of power and the violent remnants of the class-system. Smiler Washington, a sacrificial working-class scapegoat, is gradually robbed of both his spirit and individuality in the course of the play. With this and his other early plays, Wesker was recognized as a powerful voice in post-war British theatre. His skill as a playwright lies in the creation of convincing, realistic characters and dramatic situations that convey his political and social message.

Smiler's torrential speech, probably delivered on a desolate roadway not far from the military base he's just left behind, really has to be aimed at a target. All his pent up rage, frustration and indignation finally issue forth. Because the diatribe is so complete and so long, the actor must be careful not to damage his voice by shouting uncontrollably. Use the long vowels in the words to help smooth the passage of the cries and screams. You have to divide this speech into clusters and recover breath before launching into each new section. As a result of his sudden release from confinement, Smiler's state of mind ranges from jubilation to a disturbing form of hysteria. In his preparation, the actor should make choices about where this speech is taking place, what time of day or night it is, whether cars are passing by. The substitute images you conjure up can serve as targets for Smiler's rage. The character has just come through a brutal ordeal which has left its marks. The speech is about freedom and fear.

Cloud Nine
(1979) Caryl Churchill

Act 2, scene 2. A London park in the Spring of 1979.

Gerry (20–30) is Edward's lover. Edward's domesticity and 'wifely' abasement increasingly frustrate Gerry. He loves Edward but also pursues an independent and promiscuous lifestyle on the sly.

GERRY. [I didn't ask you to come. (EDWARD *goes*.)] Two years I've been with Edward. You have to get away sometimes or you lose sight of yourself. The train from Victoria to Clapham still has those compartments without a corridor. As soon as I got on the platform I saw who I wanted. Slim hips, tense shoulders, trying not to look at anyone. I put my hand on my packet just long enough so that he couldn't miss it. The train came in. You don't want to get in too fast or some straight dumbo might get in with you. I sat by the window. I couldn't see where the fuck he'd got to. Then just as the whistle went he got in. Great. It's a six-minute journey so you can't start anything you can't finish. I stared at him and he unzipped his flies, then he stopped. So I stood up and took my cock out. He took me in his mouth and shut his eyes tight. He was sort of mumbling it about as if he wasn't sure what to do, so I said, 'A bit tighter son' and he said 'Sorry' and then got on with it. He was jerking off with his left hand, and I could see he'd got a fairsized one. I wished he'd kept still so I could see his watch. I was getting really turned on. What if we pulled into Clapham Junction now. Of course by the time we sat down again the train was just slowing up. I felt wonderful. Then he started talking.

It's better if nothing is said. Once you find he's a librarian in Walthamstow with a special interest in science fiction and lives with his aunt, then forget it. He said I hope you don't think I do this all the time. I said I hope you will from now on. He said he would if I was on the train, but why don't we go out for a meal? I opened the door before the train stopped. I told him I lived with somebody. I don't want to know. He was jogging sideways to keep up. He said 'What's your phone number, you're my ideal physical type, what sign of the zodiac are you? Where do you live? Where are you going now?' It's not fair, I saw him at Victoria a couple of months later and I went straight down to the end of the platform and I picked up somebody really great who never said a word, just smiled.

COMMENTARY: When it first appeared in London and New York, Caryl Churchill's *Cloud Nine* made an instant impact. It is a play about sexual fantasies fulfilled and unfulfilled; the reversals of history and genders. The lines of conflict are clearly drawn between the anxiety of staying within a defined social role and the liberation experienced when stereotyped guises are suddenly dropped.

This particular speech, a graphic and oddly good-humoured description of a sex act on a train, reflects a gleeful promiscuity that a post-AIDS play, like Tony Kushner's *Angels in America*, might now handle in a very different manner. What makes this monologue so good is the way it tells a complete story without missing a beat. Nothing, literally, is left to the imagination. Notice, though, the loneliness it signals and the facelessness of the other man. The brief encounter between strangers on a train is as impersonal an act as having a ticket punched. This is a world where actions speak louder than words. Words, in fact, would only get in the way of quick pleasure. The actor must use flirtatious suspense to lead the audience on and make them voyeurs of the tryst.

Curse of the Starving Class
(1976) Sam Shepard

Act 1. A kitchen in a run-down farmhouse in rural California.

Wesley (20s) lives with his parents and younger sister on a derelict farm that will soon be up for sale. He wears 'sweatshirt, jeans and cowboy boots'. His father, in a drunken stupor, breaks into the house during the night and his mother calls in the police, fearing for her life. As the play opens the next morning, Wesley is clearing up the debris from the door smashed by his father. Wesley sullenly snaps at his mother, resentful that she had to call in the police. He shows more concern for his own 'humiliation' than for his mother's situation. After an uneasy silence Wesley starts this speech.

WESLEY (*as he throws wood into wheelbarrow*). I was lying there on my back. I could smell the avocado blossoms. I could hear the coyotes. I could hear stock cars squealing down the street. I could feel myself in my bed in my room in this house in this town in this state in this country. I could feel this country close like it was part of my bones. I could feel the presence of all the people outside, at night, in the dark. Even sleeping people I could feel. Even all the sleeping animals. Dogs. Peacocks. Bulls. Even tractors sitting in the wetness, waiting for the sun to come up. I was looking straight up at the ceiling at all my model airplanes hanging by all their thin metal wires. Floating. Swaying very quietly like they were being blown by someone's breath. Cobwebs moving with them. Dust laying on their wings. Decals peeling off their wings. My P-39. My Messerschmitt. My Jap Zero. I could feel myself lying far below them on my bed like I was on the ocean and overhead they were on reconnais-

48

sance. Scouting me. Floating. Taking pictures of the enemy. Me, the enemy. I could feel the space around me like a big, black world. I listened like an animal. My listening was afraid. Afraid of sound. Tense. Like any second something could invade me. Some foreigner. Something undescribable. Then I heard the Packard coming up the hill. From a mile off I could tell it was the Packard by the sound of the valves. The lifters have a sound like nothing else. Then I could picture my Dad driving it. Shifting unconsciously. Downshifting into second for the last pull up the hill. I could feel the headlights closing in. Cutting through the orchard. I could see the trees being lit one after the other by the lights, then going back to black. My heart was pounding. Just from my Dad coming back. Then I heard him pull the brake. Lights go off. Key's turned off. Then a long silence. Him just sitting in the car. Just sitting. I picture him just sitting. What's he doing? Just sitting. Waiting to get out. Why's he waiting to get out? He's plastered and can't move. He's plastered and doesn't want to move. He's going to sleep there all night. He's slept there before. He's woken up with dew on the hood before. Freezing headache. Teeth covered with peanuts. Then I hear the door of the Packard open. A pop of metal. Dogs barking down the road. Door slams. Feet. Paper bag being tucked under one arm. Paper bag covering 'Tiger Rose'. Feet coming. Feet walking toward the door. Feet stopping. Heart pounding. Sound of door not opening. Foot kicking door. Man's voice. Dad's voice. Dad calling Mom. No answer. Foot kicking. Foot kicking harder. Wood splitting. Man's voice. In the night. Foot kicking hard through door. One foot right through door. Bottle crashing. Glass breaking. Fist through door. Man cursing. Man going insane. Feet and hands tearing. Head smashing. Man yelling. Shoulder smashing. Whole body crashing. **Woman screaming. Mom screaming. Mom screaming for police. Man throwing wood. Man throwing** up. Mom calling cops. Dad crashing away. Back down driveway. Car door slamming. Ignition grinding. Wheels screaming. First gear grinding. Wheels screaming off down hill. Packard disappearing. Sound disappearing. No sound. No sight. Mom crying soft. Soft crying. Then no sound. Then softly crying. Then moving around through house. Then no moving. Then crying softly. Then stopping. Then, far off the freeway could be heard. (WESLEY *picks up one end of the wheelbarrow. He makes the sound of a car and pushes it off right.*)

COMMENTARY: *Curse of the Starving Class* is a quintessential Sam Shepard play: poetically clipped and richly textured. Shepard creates a highly imagistic drama that shows a stark, gloomy vision of the stereotypical American experience of happiness and plenty. All of his characters are in some way starved: emotionally, spiritually and materially. They hunger for a connection they can never seem to make.

Wesley delivers this speech whilst in the act of cleaning-up the stage. The shattered doorway is a significant prop. His physical actions punctuate the dialogue that is delivered like a recorded dream: image piled upon image. One of Shepard's techniques is to use narration like the eye of a motion picture camera or the microphone of a tape recorder; a mixture of tracking shots, stills and close-up combines with various acoustics to create the image. Think of the speech as being like a reel of film or a tape of sound. When performing this speech, the actor must remember that he is editing action and experience for the audience. Try to capture the narrative episodes of the story then hold them to make them clear for the audience as they watch and listen. Don't hustle through the speech. Each sentence must stay focused on a single object or incident. The sheer accumulation and play between these elements give the speech its power and rhythm. Notice especially how distance is contracted in the monologue: sound begins far away on the plains and the highway and gradually moves into the yard and finally into the house. All of the character's senses are brought into play: sound, smell, sight and Wesley's curious kind of animal instinct. In many ways Wesley is like a preternatural night creature with an awareness that passes all understanding. Yet he is reporting what he has experienced quite neutrally and without emotion; like a dog who can sense the oncoming event long before a human can and then sits and watches it happen.

A Day in the Death of Joe Egg

(1967) Peter Nichols

Act 1. In front of the stage and to the audience.

Bri 'is thirty-three but looks younger. Hardly ever at rest, acts being maladroit but the act is skilful. Clowning may give way to ineffectual hectoring and then self-piteous gloom'. He is a schoolteacher and married to Sheila. They have a ten-year-old spastic daughter – nicknamed Joe Egg by Bri. Caring for Joe tends to dominate their lives; to help cope they devise an elaborate series of fantasy scenarios and games involving Joe, treating her as if she were only a two-year-old. This helps make their tragic situation bearable. However, the strain of all this is beginning to take its toll on their marriage. Bri opens the play with this speech, which he directs at the audience.

BRI. That's enough! (*Pause. Almost at once, louder.*) I said enough! (*Pause. Stares at audience.*) Another word and you'll all be here till five o'clock. Nothing to me, is it? I've got all the time in the world. (*Moves across without taking his eyes off them.*) I didn't even get to the end of the corridor before there was such a din all the other teachers started opening their doors as much as to say what the hell's going on there's SOMEBODY TALKING NOW! (*Pause, stares again, like someone facing a mad dog.*) Who was it? You? You, Mister Man? . . . I did not *accuse* you, I *asked* you. Someone in the back row? (*Stares dumbly for some seconds. Relaxes, moves a few steps. Shrugs.*) You're the losers, not me. Who's that? (*Turns on them again.*) Right – hands on heads! Come on, that includes you, put the comb away. Eyes front and sit up. All of you, sit up! (*Puts his own hands on his head for a while, watching for a move, waiting for a sound, then takes them down.*
52

Suddenly roars.) Hands on head and eyes front! YOU I'm talking to! You'll be *tired* by the time I've finished. Stand on your seat. And keep your hands on your heads. Never mind what's going on outside, that joker at the back. Keep looking out here. Eyes front, hands on head. (*Moves across. Bell rings*.) Who said MOVE? Nobody said move. Hands on heads . . . Next one to groan stands on the seat. We're going to have one minute's perfect silence before you go. (*Looks at his watch*.) If we have to wait till midnight. (*Stands watching for some seconds*.) That's nice. I like that. Now try to hold it just like that till I get to this machine-gun over here. (*Moves upstage, turning his back. Turns back at once*.) My fault, all right. Little joke. No more laughing. Eyes front, hands on heads. (*Waits for silence, looks at watch, moving across suddenly looks up, very cross again*.) Who was that? Whoever did – that – can open the window before we all get gassed . . . Wait a minute! Three of you? What are you – a group? One go – one nearest the window. All the others, eyes front, hands on heads. Right. (*Looks at watch*.) That characteristic performance from our friend near the window means we return to Go. (*Looks up sharply*.) Shall I make it *two* minutes? (*Looks down again. Ten seconds pass*.) We could have had this sooner. Then we shouldn't be wasting time sitting here when we might be . . . well . . . let's all – think – what we might be doing – 'stead of sitting here when the rest have all gone home – we could be . . . (*Speaking quietly now, absently staring into space. Few more seconds pass. When he speaks again, it is as if in a reverie*.) Yes – eyes front . . . hands on breasts . . . STOP the laughter! WHO wants to start another minute? (*Looks at watch then up again*.) And whatever the great joke is, whatever it is that has so tickled your Stone Age sense of humour – when all my efforts have failed . . . save it till you're outside. I'm going to get my coat from the staff-room now. And you will be as quiet as mice –

no, fish – till I get back. All right? I don't want to hear a sound. Not a bubble. (*Goes off.*)

COMMENTARY: Peter Nichols' tragicomedy, *A Day in the Death of Jo Egg*, has had a wealth of productions in theatres all over the world and was made into a film in 1972, with Alan Bates in the role of Bri. The play presents a lacerating portrait of a marriage stretched to breaking point by the trauma of having to cope with a spastic child who is dying a little bit more each day. Nichols deals with this difficult subject by balancing rich humour with deep compassion.

Bri is a restless and voluble man. One imagines that he can never stop pacing or talking. He opens his speech like a schoolmaster disciplining his class but also acts like a comedian talking back to an audience of hecklers. The effect is openly confrontational, making this a natural audition speech. The actor has to keep changing his focus as he picks on separate members of the audience. Apart from its comic and menacing possibilities, the speech also discloses Bri's nervous paranoia and suspicions. The actor must remember that the character has a situation at home he cannot control: a spastic child who commands every ounce of his patience and control. Here onstage, alone, Bri can release. He can be the centre of attention for a change and feel in charge. Before long he has the whole audience engaged in a 'Simple Simon' hands-on-head routine. It is a silly and childish routine but also a madcap and desperate one. This speech demands acting that is daring, threatening and entertaining.

East

(1975) Steven Berkoff

Scene 16. A bare stage. Les's Speech: A Night Out.

Les (18–20) is from the East End of London. He is a member of a youth gang.

LES. I fancy going down the Lyceum tonight. . . . I double fancy that. . . . Being as it's Sunday we'll have Mr Ted Heath the famous band leader, not the acid bath murderer or notorious political impersonator-cum-week-end transvestite – and Dicky Valentine in a blue gabardine, button 2, flap pockets, hip length whistle and flute. I'll wear a roll away collar, a Johnny Ray collar, that sails out of your necks and a skinny tie – a slim Jim. French cuffs on the trousers with a 15 inch bottom. What about that handsome Donegal tweed with DB lapels? Button one, patch pockets, dropped loops, cross pockets on the trousers, satin lined, 18 inch slit up the arse on the jacket, skirted waist. What that one? Er – yeah – it's beautiful – fingertip length velvet collar, plenty of pad in the chest ('Come on Morry I said, more padding'). Of course when we were geary we pulled – not all slags neither, but you need wheels – no point in pulling without wheels – or you'd end up taking some scrubber down Edmonton and walking all the way back to Commercial Road at three in the morning with as often as not, nothing to show for it except a J. Arthur reluctantly given at the point of a seven inch honed and sharpened shiv menacing her jugular. When we got our wheels we pulled handsomely a much better quality of cunt. There was not much good quality cunt about then. And most of it were from Billingsgate.

COMMENTARY: *East* is a play that Steven Berkoff wrote as a homage to his youth in London's East End. Within this vibrant, anarchic comedy is a cry of revolt against waste and frustration. It seethes with passion, violence and anger. The lippy language captures the flair of youth argot with its references to hipster fashion, in-spots and in-words. Berkoff's dynamic characters are full of energy but have nowhere to go. Their articulateness is like a whirlwind spiralling in on itself.

Attempt this speech only if you really connect with its themes and style. It is the sort of speech that performs you as much as you perform it and you really must allow yourself to follow its flow. Steven Berkoff describes the performance style for this speech as follows: 'The acting has to be loose and smacking of danger . . . it must smart and whip out like a fairy's wicked lash. There is no reserve and therefore no embarrassment.' In the language there is 'cross-fertilisation with Shakespeare' with a 'few classical allusions'. Berkoff also indicates the speech can be done most effectively with either an East End (London) or Lower East Side (New York) accent. In other words, this is highly urban speech, full of the syncopated rhythms of the city streets. The sound of the words evokes their sense. Notice how much action is called for and the journey that the character makes within the speech. All the places are specific to London's East End. The performance requires good pacing since the monologue is written to sound something like a song. Les is like some eighteenth-century dandy, for him clothes and a good night out are what life is all about. He's dead earnest and very particular when it comes to selecting articles of clothing. This is a tremendously physical speech and the conceit is that it takes place partly in a men's haberdashery shop. Throughout the speech Les is sizing up the way he will look in the various 'threads' presented to him. Midway in the speech the monologue transforms into dialogue and the character starts talking to himself.

Entertaining Mr Sloane
(1964) Joe Orton

Act 2. The lounge of a suburban house. Morning.

Sloane (20) rents a room in the house of Kath and her father, Kemp. He has dyed blond hair and wears leather trousers with a white T-shirt. His own immediate satisfaction is his sole goal and this gives him a brazen confidence. He is an orphan who has grown up in an institutional home. Once a year he pays a visit to his parents' grave and, taking sandwiches with him, he makes 'a day of it'. Sloane allows Kath to seduce him, quickly becoming her lover. He also acts as chauffeur to Kath's homosexual brother, Ed, who also has a sexual interest in him. Sexual tension develops among the three of them as Sloane plays brother and sister off against one another. Kemp accuses Sloane of the murder of his old boss. Here Sloane explains to Kemp how he 'accidentally' killed the man.

SLOANE. I trust you, Pop. Listen. Keep quiet. (*Silence.*) It's like this see. One day I leave the Home. Stroll along. Sky blue. Fresh air. They'd found me a likeable permanent situation. Canteen facilities. Fortnight's paid holiday. Over-time? Time and a half after midnight. A staff dance each year. What more could one wish to devote one's life to? I certainly loved that place. The air round Twickenham was like wine. Then one day I take a trip to the old man's grave. Hic Jacets in profusion. Ashes to Ashes. Alas the fleeting. The sun was declining. A few press-ups on a tomb belonging to a family name of Cavaneagh, and I left the graveyard. I thumbs a lift from a geezer who promises me a bed. Gives me a bath. And a meal. Very friendly. All you could wish he was, a photographer. He shows me one or two experimental

57

studies. An experience for the retina and no mistake. He wanted to photo me. For certain interesting features I had that he wanted the exclusive right of preserving. You know how it is. I didn't like to refuse. No harm in it I suppose. But then I got to thinking . . . I knew a kid once called MacBride that happened to. Oh, yes . . . so when I gets to think of this I decide I got to do something about it. And I gets up in the middle of the night looking for the film see. He has a lot of expensive equipment about in his studio see. Well it appears that he gets the wrong idea. Runs in. Gives a shout. And the long and the short of it is I loses my head which is a thing I never ought to a done with the worry of them photos an all. And I hits him. I hits him. (*Pause.*) He must have had a weak heart. Something like that I should imagine. Definitely should have seen his doctor before that. I wasn't to know was I? I'm not to blame.

COMMENTARY: Joe Orton's *Entertaining Mr Sloane* deals with manipulation and menace. Orton's plays are set in a world where guilt and responsibility have vanished. Like Genet's macabre plays (*see page 92*) Orton's anarchic farces test the limits of amorality. The faintly anonymous Sloane – with his dyed hair and outfit that is nothing more than a costume – is a character with an undisclosed past. Who is he? What are his sexual preferences? Has he really killed someone? What he tells us is what we get. It is the actor's job to convince the audience of the truth and so reveal some part of the character's centre.

Sloane, as this speech exposes, is a drifter; a true orphan, a symbol of amorality. Sex for him is a dispassionate transaction and the persona he adopts in the play is that of a male hustler. He moves from encounter to encounter without rhyme or reason. His life is little more than a series of brief encounters with faceless strangers. His world is curiously loveless and bleak. Notice that he uses simple images when he speaks, defining the world through its colour and texture. You could compare his existence to a series of quickly taken snapshots. Photography and, by association, pornography provide some of the speech's central images. Notice that Sloane is never overtly graphic, he insinuates by implication. He chooses his words carefully; the compromising pornographic photographs are 'experimental studies . . . of certain interesting features'. In acting this speech you simply flash the images at the audience in a teasing manner. There is nothing here to dwell upon or to commit to emotionally. Sloane is a cold, dangerous fish who uses sexuality as an enticement.

Faith Healer
(1979) Brian Friel

Part One. A hall set up with three rows of chairs. On the backdrop is a tatty sign: 'The Fantastic Francis Hardy. Faith Healer. One Night Only.'

Francis Hardy is 'middle-aged; grey or greying; pale, lined face. The overcoat is unbuttoned, the collar up at the back; either navy or black, and of heavy-nap material; a good coat once but now shabby, stained, slept-in. Underneath he is wearing a dark suit that is polished with use; narrow across the shoulders; sleeves and legs too short. A soiled white shirt. A creased tie. Vivid green socks.' In this opening monologue he reflects on how he became a faith healer.

FRANK. Faith healer – faith healing. A craft without an apprenticeship, a ministry without responsibility, a vocation without a ministry. How did I get involved? As a young man I chanced to flirt with it and it possessed me. No, no, no, no, no – that's rhetoric. No; let's say I did it . . . because I could do it. That's accurate enough. And occasionally it worked – oh, yes, occasionally it *did* work. Oh, yes. And when it did, when I stood before a man and placed my hands on him and watched him become whole in my presence, those were nights of exultation, of consummation – no, not that I was doing good, giving relief, spreading joy – good God, no nothing at all to do with that; but because the questions that undermined my life then became meaningless and because I knew that for those few hours I had become whole in myself, and perfect in myself, and in a manner of speaking, an aristocrat, if the term doesn't offend you. But the questionings, the questionings . . . They began modestly enough with the pompous struttings of a young man: *Am I endowed with a unique and awesome gift?* – my God, yes, I'm afraid so. And I suppose the other extreme was *Am I a con man?* – which of course was nonsense, I think. And between those absurd exaggerations the possibilities were legion. Was it all chance? – or skill? – or illusion? – or delusion? Precisely what power did I possess? Could I summon it? When and how? Was I its servant? Did it reside in my ability to invest someone with faith in me or did I evoke from him a healing faith in himself? Could my healing be effected without faith? But faith in what? – in me? – in the possibility? – faith in faith? And is the power diminishing? You're beginning to masquerade, aren't you? You're becoming a husk, aren't you? And so it went on and on and on. Silly, wasn't it? Considering that nine times out of ten nothing at all happened. But they persisted right to the end, those nagging, tormenting, maddening questions that rotted my life. When I refused to confront them, they ambushed me. And when they threatened to submerge me, I silenced them with whiskey. That was efficient for a while. It got me through the job night after night. And when nothing happened or when something did happen, it helped me to accept that. But I can tell you this: there was one thing I did know, one thing I always knew right from the beginning – I always knew, drunk or sober, I always knew when nothing was going to happen.

COMMENTARY: Brian Friel's *Faith Healer* is an incantatory, poetic drama in which three characters tell differing versions of the same tragic events through four interlocking monologues. It is a play about desolation and failure. The speeches, when acted effectively and truthfully, sound like dreams retold. The exact order of events is always left in doubt. Throughout the play there is no attempt to create a fourth wall, so what the characters say, by way of heartbreaking confession, must be shared openly and intimately with the audience as though they sit in judgement. Francis Hardy, the central character, begins and closes the play. This speech is but a section of his opening monologue.

Frank is a ghostly presence who stands before the audience as a tragic bard exhumed from the grave. His narration comes in wave after wave of lyrical reminiscence, which he intones like a secular sermon. The monologue also has a confessional quality. It is essential that the actor creates a strong rapport with his listeners. Frank is explaining to the audience that he is not a fraud but a true faith healer. Laying on of hands is his gift. Charisma is his stock in trade. Language is his tool. Frank is cursed by the gift: sometimes it works sometimes not. He might resemble either Christ or a charlatan. The monologue is also like a defence speech. Frank leaves it up to the audience to decide how much of what he says is true. Each sentence has a clear rhythm and lilt, and this can help propel the actor through this garrulous, questioning speech. It works best if you build slowly. Frank is also an alcoholic. The playwright makes it clear that Francis Hardy is not your ordinary drunk but a shabby saint with a guilty past that keeps surfacing. His intoxication with words keeps him talking.

The Glass Menagerie
(1945) Tennessee Williams

Scene 7. The Wingfield apartment in St Louis during the Depression.

Jim O'Connor (25) is a 'nice, ordinary, young man'. He works with Tom Wingfield in a warehouse as a shipping clerk. Tom invites Jim home to meet his sister, Laura. Laura and Jim attended high school together. She 'liked' him but he barely remembers her. At school he was a 'hero', showing 'astonishing' promise, but since graduating he has not fulfilled his early potential – and he is all too aware of his failure. Jim is friendly and outgoing. Laura is partially crippled and painfully shy. She retreats into an imaginary world inhabited by her delicate collection of glass animals. In this scene Jim attempts to draw Laura out. When he tries dancing with her he accidentally knocks over and breaks her most precious glass animal – a unicorn. Jim, finding himself touched by Laura's prettiness and delicacy, kisses her and she 'sinks on the sofa with a bright, dazed look'. This speech follows on from that moment as he awkwardly realizes the implications of that kiss.

JIM. Stumblejohn! I shouldn't have done that – that was way off the beam. You don't smoke, do you? (*She looks up, smiling, not hearing the question. He sits beside her rather gingerly. She looks at him speechlessly – waiting. He coughs decorously and moves a little farther aside as he considers the situation and senses her feelings, dimly, with perturbation. He speaks gently.*) Would you – care for a – mint? (*She doesn't seem to hear him but her look grows brighter even.*) Peppermint? Life Saver? My pocket's a regular drugstore – wherever I go . . . (*He pops a mint in his mouth. Then he gulps and decides to make a clean breast of it. He speaks slowly and gingerly.*)

63

Laura, you know, if I had a sister like you, I'd do the same thing as Tom. I'd bring out fellows and – introduce her to them. The right type of boys – of a type to – appreciate her. Only – well – he made a mistake about me. Maybe I've got no call to be saying this. That may not have been the idea in having me over. But what if it was? There's nothing wrong about that. The only trouble is that in my case – I'm not in a situation to – do the right thing. I can't take down your number and say I'll phone. I can't call up next week and – ask for a date. I thought I had better explain the situation in case you – misunderstood it and – I hurt your feelings. . . . (*There is a pause. Slowly, very slowly,* LAURA's *look changes, her eyes returning slowly from his to the glass figure in her palm.* . . .)

[LAURA (*faintly*). You – won't – call again?

No, Laura, I can't.] (*He rises from the sofa.*) As I was just explaining, I've – got strings on me. Laura, I've – been going steady! I go out all the time with a girl named Betty. She's a home-girl like you, and Catholic, and Irish, and in a great many ways we – get along fine. I met her last summer on a moonlight boat trip up the river to Alton, on the *Majestic*. Well – right away from the start it was – love! (LAURA *sways slightly forward and grips the arm of the sofa. He fails to notice, now enrapt in his own comfortable being.*) Being in love has made a new man of me! (*Leaning stiffly forward, clutching the arm of the sofa,* LAURA *struggles visibly with her storm. But* JIM *is oblivious; she is a long way off.*) The power of love is really pretty tremendous! Love is something that – changes the whole world, Laura! (*The storm abates a little and* LAURA *leans back. He notices her again.*) It happened that Betty's aunt took sick, she got a wire and had to go to Centralia. So Tom – when he asked me to dinner – I naturally just accepted the invitation, not knowing that you – that he – that I – (*He stops awkwardly.*) Huh – I'm a stumblejohn!

COMMENTARY: Tennessee Williams' *The Glass Menagerie*, with its delicate illusions always on the verge of being shattered, is one of the best-wrought American dramas. The play reveals the past as a potent memory full of dreams and nostalgia, pain and regret. Williams evokes an atmospheric stage world and peoples it with characters who invite compassion and sympathy from the audience. This is Tennessee Williams' most consciously autobiographical play and was his first great success in the theatre.

This speech is one long compensation for a misjudged kiss. Jim is the 'gentleman caller' that the Wingfield family has been anticipating, but he proves not to be quite the knight in shining armour that Laura's domineering mother, Amanda, was hoping he would be. Like the other characters in the play, Jim has a strong sense of a more resonant past, a time of former glory. He has an engagingly naive and direct quality, but none of the refinements of a Southern 'gentleman caller'. He's an average guy whose awkwardness is signalled at the start and end of the speech in the phrase 'stumblejohn'. When he breaks Laura's prized glass unicorn (a major moment in the drama) he symbolically shatters the fragile illusion upon which her dreams rest. Laura's silence and then her single, frightened line prompts him to confess that he has a girlfriend. Unthinkingly he now breaks Laura's illusions for a second time. Williams provides the actor with detailed signposts in his stage directions and they will help guide you through the emotional shifts in the speech. Jim is not naturally articulate but when he is confronted with Laura's silence he is forced to find the words to deal with an embarrassing and delicate situation. This whole speech must be performed as if you were treading carefully over broken glass but trying to sweep it up at the same time.

The Homecoming
(1965) Harold Pinter

Act 2. An old house in North London. A summer afternoon.

Lenny (early 30s) lives with his brother Joey, an aspiring boxer and their elderly father Max and his brother Sam. Lenny's 'occupation' is as a small-time pimp. Unexpectedly his older brother Teddy arrives home in the middle of the night to introduce his wife Ruth to the family. Teddy has made good in the United States where he is a professor of philosophy. There is considerable ambiguity, menace and tension between all members of the family. They warily protect their own territory and possessions. Ruth, as the only female, adds a new provocative and sexual dimension to the curt relations in this all-male household. One by one they slowly try to take control of Ruth. Their threats are verbal rather than physical. This speech follows a scene in which Teddy has just admitted eating Lenny's cheese roll.

LENNY. Barefaced audacity. (*Pause.*) What led you to be so . . . vindictive against your own brother? I'm bowled over. (*Pause.*) Well, Ted, I would say this is something approaching the naked truth, isn't it? It's a real cards on the table stunt. I mean, we're in the land of no holds barred now. Well, how else can you interpret it? To pinch your younger brother's specially made cheese roll when he's out doing a spot of work, that's not equivocal, it's unequivocal. (*Pause.*) Mind you, I will say you do seem to have grown a bit sulky during the last six years. A bit sulky. A bit inner. A bit less forthcoming. It's funny, because I'd have thought that in the United States of America, I mean with the sun and all that, the open spaces, on the old campus, in your position, lecturing, in the centre of all the intellectual life out

66

there, on the old campus, all the social whirl, all the stimulation of it all, all your kids and all that, to have fun with, down by the pool, the Greyhound buses and all that, tons of iced water, all the comfort of those Bermuda shorts and all that, on the old campus, no time of the day or night you can't get a cup of coffee or a Dutch gin, I'd have thought you'd have grown more forthcoming, not less. Because I want you to know that you set a standard for us, Teddy. Your family looks up to you, boy, and you know what it does? It does its best to follow the example you set. Because you're a great source of pride to us. That's why we were so glad to see you come back, to welcome you back to your birthplace. That's why. (*Pause.*) No, listen, Ted, there's no question that we live a less rich life here than you do over there. We live a closer life. We're busy, of course. Joey's busy with his boxing, I'm busy with my occupation, Dad still plays a good game of poker, and he does the cooking as well, well up to his old standard, and Uncle Sam's the best chauffeur in the firm. But nevertheless we do make up a unit, Teddy, and you're an integral part of it. When we all sit round the backyard having a quiet gander at the night sky, there's always an empty chair standing in the circle, which is in fact yours. And so when you at length return to us, we do expect a bit of grace, a bit of *je ne sais quoi*, a bit of generosity of mind, a bit of liberality of spirit, to reassure us. We do expect that. But do we get it? Have we got it? Is that what you've given us?

COMMENTARY: Harold Pinter's *The Homecoming* is a disturbing and enigmatic comedy, revealing a family battling over territorial rights. It is one of Pinter's most theatrically effective plays. This is a world in which things are not quite as they seem, where there is mystery and menace in the mundane. The dramatic language is richly textured, full of words echoing with innuendo and invective. In this theatrical riddle Pinter, who trained as an actor himself, creates challenging, highly actable roles. A recent revival by the play's original director, Peter Hall, showed that Pinter's unique mixture of menace and humour must be carefully measured out to the audience by the performer. This speech is a classic example of the technique.

Pinter constructs the encounter between Lenny and his brother as an instance of adolescent sibling rivalry. (There are several Cain and Abel-like moments throughout the play.) A cheese roll is a trivial, laughable thing. Lenny treats its eating as both a theft and an indication of moral corruption. It is the collision of these two totally opposite values that makes the speech so simultaneously farcical and menacing. Lenny speaks in high moral tones, as if he, the street pimp, and not the better educated Teddy, was the professor of philosophy. He compounds this subversion by presenting himself as a sentimental upholder of strong family values. How much of this is done with a straight face or with tongue in cheek is up to the actor to decide. Notice how Lenny peppers his monologue with striking, inappropriate phrases like 'equivocal' and 'unequivocal'. He uses language as a front to hide behind. The actor should also notice that Pinter builds into the speech different sorts of rhythms. The actor must respect every word and every gesture. The pauses and strict punctuation should be obeyed. Short jabbing words and sentences are counterpointed by long, flowing ones. Lenny both taunts and tantalizes his brother simultaneously. Do remember that throughout the speech Teddy does not reply. His silence is a kind of threat that Lenny is attempting to deflect. Lenny looks for a reaction but never gets it. Perhaps he is frightened of his more successful and enigmatic brother.

The House of Blue Leaves
(1971) John Guare

Act 1. A shabby apartment in Sunnyside, Queens (New York). A living room filled with many lamps and pictures of movie stars and jungle animals. October 4th, 1965.

Artie Shaugnessy (45) is a zoo-keeper married to Bananas who is dottily insane. He dreams of escaping by becoming a big-time showbiz composer even though his songwriting talent does not match his ambition. His songs range from 'Where's the devil in Evelyn' to new lyrics for Irving Berlin's 'White Christmas'. His mistress, the vivaciously wacky Bunny, wants Artie to leave Bananas and marry her. Bunny's scheme is that the two of them will go to Hollywood, and Artie, with the help of his childhood friend Billy Einhorn who has become a major film producer, will be able to start on a successful songwriting career. In this scene Bunny has just forced Artie to call Billy in Hollywood to make contact after all these years. He has just placed the call through the operator and nervously waits to be connected.

ARTIE. Tattooed, baby. Tattooed. Your heart and his telephone number right on my chest like a sailor. Not you, operator. I want and fast I want in Los Angeles in Bel Air GR2–4129 and I will not dial it because I want to speak personally to my good friend and genius, Mr Billy Einhorn . . . E-I-N – don't you know how to spell it? The name of only Hollywood's leading director my friend and you better not give this number to any of your friends and call him up and bother him asking for screen tests . . . My number is RA1–2276 and don't go giving that number away and I want a good connection. . . . Hang on, Bunny – (*She takes his extended hand.*) you can hear the beepbeepbeeps – we're travelling across the country – hang on! Ring. It's ringing.

Ring. . . . Ring. It's up. Hello? Billy? Yes, operator, get off – that's Billy. Will you get off – (*To* BUNNY.) I should've called station-to-station. He picked it right up and everything. Billy! This is Ramon Navarro! . . . no, Billy, it's Artie Shaughnessy. Artie. No, New York! Did I wake you up! Can you hear me? Billy, hello! I got to tell you something – first of all, I got to tell you how bad I feel about Georgina dying – the good die young – what can I say? – and second, since you, you old bum, never come back to your old stomping grounds – your happy hunting grounds, I'm thinking of coming to see you . . . I know you can fix up a tour of the studios and that'd be great . . . and you can get us hotel reservations – that's just fine. . . . But Billy, I'm thinking I got to get away – not just a vacation – but make a change, get a break if you know what I'm getting at. . . . Bananas is fine. She's right here. We were just thinking about you – NO, IT'S NOT FINE. Billy, this sounds cruel to say, but Bananas is as dead for me as Georgina is for you. I'm in love with a remarkable, wonderful girl – yeah, she's here too – who I should've married years ago – no, we didn't know her years ago – I only met her two months ago – yeah. (*Secretively, pulling the phone off to the corner.*) It's kind of funny, a chimpanzee knocked me in the back and kinked my back out of whack and I went to this health club to work it out and in the steam section with all the steam I got lost and I went into this steam room and there was Bunny – yeah, just towels – I mean you could make a movie out of this, it was so romantic – she couldn't see me and she started talking about the weight she had to take off and the food she had to give up and she started talking about duckling with orange sauce and oysters baked with spinach and shrimps baked in the juice of melted sturgeon eyes which caviar comes from – well, you know me and food and I got so excited and the steam's getting thicker and thicker and I ripped off my towel and kind of raped her . . . and she was quiet for a long time
70

and then she finally said one of the greatest lines of all time. . . . She said, 'There's a man in here. . . .' And she was in her sheet like a toga and I was all toga'd up and I swear, Billy, we were gods and goddesses and the steam bubbled up and swirled and it was Mount Olympus. I'm a new man, Billy – a new man – and I got to make a start before it's too late and I'm calling you, crawling on my hands and knees – (BUNNY *touches him.*) no, not like that, I'm standing up straight and talking to my best buddy and saying, 'Can I come see you and bring Bunny and talk over old times?' . . . I'll pay my own way. I'm not asking you for nothing. Just your friendship. I think about you so much and I read about you in the columns and 'Conduct of Life' is playing at the Museum of Modern Art next week and I get nervous calling you and that Doris Day pic – well, Bunny and I fell out of our loge seats – no, Bananas couldn't see it – she don't go out of the house much. . . . I get nervous about calling you because, well, you know, and I'm not asking for an Auld Lang Syne treatment, but it must be kind of lonely with Georgina gone and we sent five dollars in to the Damon Runyon Cancer Fund like Walter Winchell said to do and we're gonna send more and it must be kind of lonely and the three of us – Bunny and you and me – could have some laughs. What do you say? You write me and let me know your schedule and we can come anytime. But soon. Okay, buddy? Okay? No, this is my call. I'm paying for this call so you don't have to worry – talking to you I get all opened up. You still drinking rye? Jack Daniels! Set out the glasses – open the bottle – no, I'll bring the bottle – we'll see you soon. Good night, Billy. (*The call is over.*) Soon, Billy. Soon. Soon. (*Hangs up.*)

COMMENTARY: John Guare's *House of Blue Leaves* is a surreal tragicomedy about a family of lost dreamers adrift in a world of topsy-turvy values. The play mixes the Kaufman and Hart tradition of American stage comedy with a drama of modern psychological angst. Its brilliant evocation of stand-up comedy, vaudevillian slapstick and troubled states of mind make it an acting *tour de force*. The mood of the acting changes constantly. Guare has created some of the most memorable oddball characters in modern American drama. On the surface they appear to be cartoons. Underneath, however, they reveal needs and wants as great as any tragic hero or heroine of classical drama.

Telephone monologues should on the whole be avoided. This one is an exception to that rule as it provides the actor with a zesty, viable dramatic scenario. Artie is having a two- and sometimes three-way conversation (with Bunny, the telephone operator and Billy Einhorn). Try to focus on Billy as if he was vividly present to you and not distanced down a telephone line. The actor should pace himself so that Artie's breathless enthusiasm does not get out of control. All of Artie's New York cadences come into his speaking voice as time drops away and Artie and Billy, the two boys from Queens, relive their past. The conversation lurches forwards, as Artie interrupts himself and shifts direction. At times it is hard to tell where he is heading but the actor should always be in control of the apparent confusion. So many thoughts flood together simultaneously as the two friends try and catch up on time forever lost. Notice that Artie barely gives Billy a chance to get a word in edgeways. The different social status of the two men accounts for Artie's repeated embarrassment. Billy is a success, Artie is a failure. Yet Artie's future happiness depends on this phone call. Midway through the speech superficial exchanges suddenly turn to confessional complaints as Artie pours out his troubles. Then the speech turns to begging. Finally Artie begins to retreat but can't quite find a way to end the call easily. How decisively or reluctantly you hang up the receiver is a crucial ending to the speech. Above all, Artie's nervous energy must be given motion and passion.

Huis Clos [In Camera/No Exit]
(1944) Jean-Paul Sartre

One act. A drawing-room in Second Empire style.

Joseph Garcin (30s), a South American editor of a pacifist newspaper, has recently been killed. He deserted from the army and was shot twelve times in the chest. A valet brings him into an elegant, brightly illuminated room with neither mirrors nor windows. Here he is condemned to spend the rest of eternity with two other recently deceased characters: Estelle an attractive socialite and Inez a lesbian. A bizarre triangular relationship develops between them as jealousy and desire clash. Inez is attracted to Estelle and Estelle is attracted to Garcin. Garcin sees women merely as sexual playthings, preferring the company of men. Inez realizes that they have been brought together to serve as one another's eternal torturers: there will be no physical torments, there will just be the three of them – forever together. After challenging the others, Garcin decides he will be the first to be frank and bring his 'spectres' out into the open. Earlier on he had 'seen' his wife back on earth, waiting to discover what had happened to him. Here he watches her being given his coat.

GARCIN. I'm not a very estimable person.
[INEZ. No need to tell us that. We know you were a deserter.
GARCIN. Let that be. It's only a side-issue.] I'm here because I treated my wife abominably. That's all. For five years. Naturally, she's suffering still. There she is: the moment I mention her, I see her. It's Gomez who interests me, and it's she I see. Where's Gomez got to? For five years. There! They've given her back my things; she's sitting by the window with my coat on her knees. The coat with the twelve bullet-holes. The blood's like rust; a brown ring

73

round each hole. It's quite a museum-piece, that coat; scarred with history. And I used to wear it, fancy! . . . Now, can't you shed a tear, my love? Surely you'll squeeze one out – at last? No? You can't manage it? . . . Night after night I came home blind drunk, stinking of wine and women. She'd sat up for me, of course. But she never cried, never uttered a word of reproach. Only her eyes spoke. Big, tragic eyes. I don't regret anything. I must pay the price, but I shan't whine. . . . It's snowing in the street. Won't you cry, confound you? That woman was a born martyr, you know; a victim by vocation.

[INEZ (*almost tenderly*). Why did you hurt her like that?]

It was so easy. A word was enough to make her flinch. Like a sensitive plant. But never, never a reproach. I'm fond of teasing. I watched and waited. But no, not a tear, not a protest. I'd picked her up out of the gutter, you understand. . . . Now she's stroking the coat. Her eyes are shut and she's feeling with her fingers for the bullet-holes. What are you after? What do you expect? I tell you I regret nothing. The truth is, she admired me too much. Does that mean anything to you?

[INEZ. No. Nobody admired *me*.]

So much the better. So much the better for you. I suppose all this strikes you as very vague. Well, here's something you can get your teeth into. I brought a half-caste girl to stay in our house. My wife slept upstairs; she must have heard – everything. She was an early riser and, as I and the girl stayed in bed late, she served us our morning coffee.

[INEZ. You brute!]

Yes, a brute, if you like. But a well-beloved brute. (*A far-away look comes to his eyes.*) No, it's nothing. Only Gomez and he's not talking about *me* . . . What were you saying? Yes, a brute. Certainly. Else why should I be here?

Translation by Stuart Gilbert

COMMENTARY: Sartre's *Huis Clos* revolves around the tighly woven dissension among the three characters. They are trapped with their passions and desires in eternal conflict. In Garcin's words, 'Hell is other people'. Even when the characters describe irrelevant details, each story and image comes inexorably back to that main point: human misery is occasioned by other people. In death identities are fixed and the past is a closed book without retribution. Hell offers only the opportunity to reflect on missed opportunities; there is no longer any choice. Each character has an equal share in this claustrophobic, locked-room drama. At any given moment one or the other is the play's centre.

Garcin evokes a shift in time and place. He is a passive observer as he sees his wife learning of his own death. The actor must establish Garcin as a voyeur and he must appear to see what he describes. What he sees becomes so real for him that he tries to interject and disrupt the action. It is as if Garcin is watching the events unfold on a screen. Except that he really wants to watch another scene, so that he can hear what Gomez, his successor at the newspaper, is saying about him. Remember that Garcin is a professional journalist and expert at dispassionately reporting emotions. Notice how he exudes anger, hostility and hatred of himself and others. At times he practically spits his words out. He freely admits being cruel to his wife. Everything about her irritates him; he shows no compassion, only cynical scorn for her grief. Part of the playwright's strategy in the writing is to show how inseparable people are from each other. The actor must never let the audience doubt that his wife and Gomez are as present to him as Inez and the silent Estelle; all witnesses and accusers, each adding to Garcin's guilt and paranoia. Notice how proudly he accepts that he is a 'brute' without the slightest regret or remorse. He has to confront the fact that he is absolutely powerless to influence the impressions of those he left behind. In Hell choice and direct action are no longer possibilities. All the characters can do is react.

The Iceman Cometh
(1940) Eugene O'Neill

Act 1. The back room bar of Harry Hope's saloon on an early morning in summer, 1912.

Willie Oban 'is in his late thirties, of average height, thin. His haggard, dissipated face has a small nose, a pointed chin, blue eyes with colourless lashes and brows. His blond hair, badly in need of a cut, clings in a limp part to his skull. His eyelids flutter continually as if any light were too strong for his eyes. The clothes he wears belong to a scarecrow. They seem constructed of an inferior grade of dirty blotting paper. His shoes are even more disreputable, wrecks of imitation leather, one laced with twine, the other with a bit of wire. He has no socks, and his bare feet show through holes in the soles, with his big toes sticking out of the uppers.' He is a Harvard Law School alumnus who is a resident in Harry Hope's rooming house. During most of the first act Willie has been asleep, fitfully muttering from his nightmarish dreams and only waking to beg for another drink.

WILLIE (*he has opened his eyes . . . drunk now from the effect of the huge drink he took, and speaks with a mocking suavity*). Why omit me from your Who's Who in Dipsomania, Larry? An unpardonable slight, especially as I am the only inmate of royal blood. (*To* PARRITT – *ramblingly.*) Educated at Harvard, too. You must have noticed the atmosphere of culture here. My humble contribution. Yes, Generous Stranger – I trust you're generous – I was born in the purple, the son, but unfortunately not the heir, of the late world-famous Bill Oban, King of the Bucket Shops*. A revolution

---

*****bucket shop** an illegal saloon and gambling den that flourished during the period of Prohibition in America

deposed him, conducted by the District Attorney. He was sent into exile. In fact, not to mince matters, they locked him in the can and threw away the key. Alas, his was an adventurous spirit and pined in confinement. And so he died. Forgive these reminiscences. Undoubtedly all this is well known to you. Everyone in the world knows.

[PARRITT (*uncomfortably*). Tough luck. No, I never heard of him.]

(*Blinks at him incredulously.*) Never heard? I thought everyone in the world – Why, even at Harvard I discovered my father was well known by reputation, although that was some time before the District Attorney gave him so much unwelcome publicity. Yes, even as a freshman I was notorious. I was accepted socially with all the warm cordiality that Henry Wadsworth Longfellow would have shown a drunken Negress dancing the can-can at high noon on Brattle Street. Harvard was my father's idea. He was an ambitious man. Dictatorial, too. Always knowing what was best for me. But I did make myself a brilliant student. A dirty trick on my classmates, inspired by revenge, I fear. (*He quotes.*) 'Dear college days, with pleasure rife! The grandest gladdest days of life!' But, of course, that is a Yale hymn, and they're given to rah-rah exaggeration at New Haven. I was a brilliant student at Law School, too. My father wanted a lawyer in the family. He was a calculating man. A thorough knowledge of the law close at hand in the house to help him find fresh ways to evade it. But I discovered the loophole of whiskey and escaped his jurisdiction. (*Abruptly to* PARRITT.) Speaking of whiskey, sir, reminds me – and, I hope, reminds you – that when meeting a Prince the customary salutation is 'What'll you have?'.

COMMENTARY: O'Neill's *The Iceman Cometh* examines a colourful group of dissolute drunks and assorted hangers-on who inhabit

77

a sleazy New York bar attached to Harry Hope's rooming house. This drama helped to set the style for a range of American genre plays about dreams and disillusion. These include William Saroyan's *The Time of Your Life* and more recent perennials like Robert Patrick's *Kennedy's Children* and Lanford Wilson's *Balm in Gilead* and *Hot l Baltimore*. The free flowing liquor leads inevitably to free flowing talk; the bar-room becomes akin to a secular confessional. As the drama progresses each character has a chance to speak out, to articulate his hopes and dreams.

Willie's lost grandeur and the sins of his father are at the root of his discontent. They are a strong part of the reason why he has lost the battle with the demon drink. What is also clear, apart from Willie's inglorious fall from grace, is the potent way that Harvard Law School and Boston still loom in his life. They probably represent some sort of Golden Age of high achievement. Brahmin polish still shows through Willie's tattered state. The remnants of his education show in his boozy wit and eloquent style of speaking. He presents himself as some sort of hobo king, dispossessed royalty waiting for a second chance to regain the lost throne. Speeches by stage drunks are always hard to make work. Here the actor must strive to gather together the fragments of Willie's shattered life and present them to the audience as an urgent bit of salvaging before he falls back into his customary stupor. For just a brief moment the soul of Willie must be illuminated. The cruel, judgemental father still lies trapped inside the son.

Krapp's Last Tape
(1958) Samuel Beckett

One act. Krapp's den. A late evening in the future.

Krapp (69) is 'a wearish old man'. He wears 'rusty black narrow trousers too short for him. Rusty black sleeveless waistcoat, four capacious pockets. Heavy silver watch and chain. Grimy white shirt open at neck, no collar. Surprising pair of dirty white boots, size ten at least, very narrow and pointed. White face. Purple nose. Disordered grey hair. Unshaven. Very near-sighted (but unspectacled). Hard of hearing. Cracked voice. Distinctive intonation. Laborious walk.' He is alone in his den, which is sparsely furnished with a small table. After thirty years Krapp plays back an autobiographical tape he had recorded on his 39th birthday, hearing of a failed love affair. In this speech he starts to record a new tape updating his dreary life, detailing his failure as a lover and a writer.

KRAPP. Just been listening to that stupid bastard I took myself for thirty years ago, hard to believe I was ever as bad as that. Thank God that's all done with anyway. (*Pause.*) The eyes she had! (*Broods, realizes he is recording silence, switches off, broods. Finally.*) Everything there, everything, all the – (*Realizes this is not being recorded, switches on.*) Everything there, everything on this old muckball, all the light and dark and famine and feasting of . . . (*hesitates*) . . . the ages! (*In a shout.*) Yes! (*Pause.*) Let that go! Jesus! Take his mind off his homework! Jesus! (*Pause. Weary.*) Ah well, maybe he was right. (*Pause.*) Maybe he was right. (*Broods. Realizes. Switches off. Consults envelope.*) Pah! (*Crumples it and throws it away. Broods. Switches on.*) Nothing to say, not a squeak. What's a year now? The sour cud and the iron stool. (*Pause*.) Revelled in the word spool. (*With relish*.) Spooool! Happiest moment of the past half million. (*Pause*.) Seventeen copies sold, of which eleven at trade price to free circulating libraries beyond the seas. Getting known. (*Pause*.) One pound six and something, eight I have little doubt. (*Pause*.) Crawled out once or twice, before the summer was cold. Sat shivering in the park, drowned in dreams and burning to be gone. Not a soul. (*Pause*.) Last fancies. (*Vehemently*.) Keep 'em under! (*Pause*.) Scalded the eyes out of me reading *Effie* again, a page a day, with tears again. Effie . . . (*Pause*.) Could have been happy with her, up there on the Baltic, and the pines, and the dunes. (*Pause*.) Could I? (*Pause*.) And she? (*Pause*.) Pah! (*Pause*.) Fanny came in a couple of times. Bony old ghost of a whore. Couldn't do much, but I suppose better than a kick in the crutch. The last time wasn't so bad. How do you manage it, she said, at your age? I told her I'd been saving up for her all my life. (*Pause*.) Went to Vespers once, like when I was in short trousers. (*Pause. Sings*.)

Now the day is over.

Night is drawing nigh-igh,

Shadows – (*coughing, then almost inaudible*) – of the evening

Steal across the sky.

(*Gasping*.) Went to sleep and fell off the pew. (*Pause*.) Sometimes wondered in the night if a last effort mightn't – (*Pause*.) Ah finish your booze now and get to your bed. Go on with this drivel in the morning. Or leave it at that. (*Pause*.) Leave it at that. (*Pause*.) Lie propped up in the dark – and wander. Be again in the dingle on a Christmas Eve, gathering holly, the red-berried. (*Pause*.) Be again on Croghan on a Sunday morning, in the haze, with the bitch, stop and listen to the bells. (*Pause*.) And so on. (*Pause*.) Be again, be again. (*Pause*.) All that old misery. (*Pause*.) Once wasn't enough for you. (*Pause*.) Lie down across her.

COMMENTARY: Beckett's *Krapp's Last Tape* is one of the greatest full-length monologues written for the modern stage. The sheer accumulation of facts, ideas and emotions – at times almost unbearable – approximate an entire life lived in the concentrated space of a one-act play. Few playwrights have succeeded in making stream-of-consciousness narrative work as effectively as Beckett.

Krapp is as dusty and downtrodden as a street tramp. To be blunt about it, Krapp is afflicted with a severe case of verbal diarrhoea. He speaks in monologue to the accompaniment of his own monologue as recorded on a small tape recorder. The latter is a crucial stage prop. Through the tape the character confronts time and things past. It also conjures up reveries of things beautiful and also things better left unsaid. Beckett writes poetry in disguise so the actor should never consciously signal the lyricism inherent in the words. There is always a danger in performing Beckett that if the words gather too much momentum or get away from the actor, the audience will lose sight of the character. You must allow the audience to keep up with you. Beckett is all about character revelations spoken under extreme and controlled circumstances. The stage is like a laboratory, the character like a specimen. The desperate physical actions called for in the stage directions and the abrupt cancellations in the speech ('Pah!', 'Leave it at that', 'All that old misery') undercut the lyricism in the language. The process shows us Krapp fighting to regain control of his speech. The actor ought to present the audience with a character struggling with his own memory; a memory that relentlessly assaults him with images. What Krapp does here is speak in tongues. He shifts from voice to voice as though he were channel-hopping on a radio.

La Turista
(1967) Sam Shepard

Act 1. A hotel room in Mexico.

Kent (20s) and Salem are a young American couple on holiday in Mexico. As the play opens they are in their beds suffering from painful sunburn. Kent is also experiencing diarrhoea; the 'la turista' of the title. A young native enters their room while they are still in bed. In response to his silence they offer him handfuls of money from their suitcase, which he ignores. As Kent tries to phone the hotel manager, the boy pulls the telephone out of the wall and moves downstage to make grimacing faces at the audience. Kent confronts the boy who spits at him. Kent runs off to clean himself in the shower. Kent delivers this speech when he returns.

KENT (*he enters from the stage right door dressed in a straight brimmed Panamanian hat, a linen shirt, hand made boots, underwear, and a pistol around his waist. His skin is now pale white and should appear made up. He crosses centre stage, strutting*). Well! I feel like a new man after all that. I think I finally flushed that old amoeba right down the old drain. (*He struts up and down, hitching his pistol on his hips.*)
[BOY. Ole!]
Yes, sir! Nothing like a little amoebic dysentery to build up a man's immunity to his environment. That's the trouble with the States you know. Everything's so clean and pure and immaculate up there that a man doesn't even have a chance to build up his own immunity. They're breeding a bunch of lily livered weaklings up there simply by not having a little dirty water around to toughen people up. Before you know it them people ain't going to be able to travel nowhere outside

their own country on account of their low resistance. An isolated land of purification. That's what I'd call it. Now they got some minds, I'll grant you that. But the mind ain't nothing without the old body tagging along behind to follow things through. And the old body ain't nothing without a little amoeba.

[SALEM. Bravo!]

(SALEM and BOY *hum, 'When Johnny Comes Marching Home,' as* KENT *struts more proudly up and down and takes out the pistol and starts twirling it on his trigger finger*.) Yes, sir! That's always been true as long as man's been around on this earth and it ain't going to stop just on account of a few high falootin' ideas about comfort and leisure. No sirree! Why it'll get so bad up there that even foreigners won't be able to take the cleanliness. Their systems will act the same way in reverse. Nobody can come in and nobody can get out. An isolated land. That's what I call it.

[BOY. Bravo! Bravo!]

(KENT *gets more carried away with himself as they hum louder in the background*.) Then the next step is in-breeding in a culture like that where there's no one coming in and no one getting out. Incest! Yes sirree! The land will fall apart. Just take your Indians for example. Look what's happened to them through incest. Smaller and smaller! Shorter life span! Rotten teeth! Low resistance! The population shrinks. The people die away. Extinction! Destruction! Rot and ruin! I see it all now clearly before me! The Greatest Society on its way down hill.

COMMENTARY: Sam Shepard's great gift is his ability to create daringly combustible plays that are exercises in free-association. He collides social and political themes to achieve a unique dramatic style and vocabulary. His language flickers with life, shifting suddenly from one plane of reality to another. *La Turista* is one of his earliest stage plays, but already his taste for range roving in and around the American psyche is on full display. Shepard shows a satirical cartoonist's glee in the way he boldly portrays his native land and its people. Kent and Salem are typical tourists abroad who stupidly drink the water. They are also a couple of brand named, low-tar American cigarettes.

Notice that the speech begins, literally, with the germ of an idea. An amoeba in Kent's digestive tract gradually blooms into notions about the extinction and destruction of American society. (The playwright has often used the image of spreading disease as an analogue for the notion that there is something rotten in American life.) The challenge here for the actor is how to control the imaginative anarchy that Kent's fantasy unleashes. Like many modern dramatists Shepard is uninterested in the creation of coherent and well-rounded, psychological characters. His taste for the surreal and unexpected utterance liberates any actor to make Kent into something of his own imaginative choosing. You can push this monologue as far as you want in order to see it from the right perspective of outrageousness. One thing that you might notice in the speech is the fact that Kent comes across as an Old Testament prophet of doom and gloom. So you could think of the monologue as a kind of evangelical repentance speech. Any number of interpretations is possible.

Long Day's Journey into Night
(1940) Eugene O'Neill

Act 4. Living room of James Tyrone's summer home, 1912. Midnight.

Edmund Tyrone (23) is the younger son of Mary and James Tyrone. He 'looks like both his parents, but is more like his mother. Her big, dark eyes are the dominant feature in his long, narrow Irish face. His mouth has the same quality of hypersensitiveness hers possesses . . . but his nose is his father's and his face in profile recalls Tyrone's. . . . It is in the quality of extreme nervous sensibility that the likeness of Edmund to his mother is most marked. He is plainly in bad health.' He has returned home from years away at sea with what appears to be consumption. His father, although a successful and famous actor, favours squandering his money on worthless land deals instead of paying for reputable health care for his son and his wife. When Mary was pregnant with Edmund, Tyrone had her seen to by a quack doctor, and as a result she has been unwell and neurotic. She is also a secret morphine addict. Edmund writes for a newspaper but has aspirations to become a poet. In this scene Edmund has been confronting his father and after recriminations on both sides they retreat into the safe world of recollection and memory. During the evening they have been drinking heavily. As Edmund starts this speech they hear Mary moving in the room above them.

EDMUND (*pleads tensely*). For Christ's sake, Papa, forget it! (*He reaches out and pours a drink. TYRONE starts to protest, then gives it up. EDMUND drinks. He puts down the glass. His expression changes. When he speaks it is as if he were deliberately giving way to drunkenness and seeking to hide behind a maudlin manner.*) Yes, she moves above and beyond us, a ghost haunting the past, and here we sit pretending to forget, but straining our ears listening for the slightest sound, hearing the fog drip from the eaves like the uneven tick of a rundown, crazy clock – or like the dreary tears of a trollop spattering in a puddle of stale beer on a honky-tonk table top! (*He laughs with maudlin appreciation.*) Not so bad, that last, eh? Original, not Baudelaire. Give me credit! (*Then with alcoholic talkativeness.*) You've just told me some high spots in your memories. Want to hear mine? They're all connected with the sea. Here's one. When I was on the Squarehead rigger, bound for Buenos Aires. Full moon in the Trades. The old hooker driving fourteen knots. I lay on the bowsprit, facing astern, with the water foaming into spume under me, the masts with every sail white in the moonlight, towering high above me. I became drunk with the beauty and singing rhythm of it, and for a moment I lost myself – actually lost my life. I was set free! I dissolved in the sea, became white sails and flying spray, became beauty and rhythm, became moonlight and the ship and the high dim-starred sky! I belonged, without past or future, within peace and unity and a wild joy, within something greater than my own life, or the life of Man, to Life itself! To God, if you want to put it that way. Then another time, on the American Line, when I was lookout on the crow's nest in the dawn watch. A calm sea, that time. Only a lazy groundswell and a slow drowsy roll of the ship. The passengers asleep and none of the crew in sight. No sound of man. Black smoke pouring from the funnels behind and beneath me. Dreaming, not keeping lookout, feeling alone, and above, and apart, watching the dawn creep like a painted dream over the sky and sea which slept together. Then the moment of ecstatic freedom came. The peace, the end of the quest, the last harbour, the joy of belonging to a fulfillment beyond men's lousy, pitiful, greedy fears and hopes and dreams! And several other times in my life, when I was swimming far out, or lying alone on a beach, I have had the same experience. Became the sun, the hot sand, green seaweed anchored to a

86

rock, swaying in the tide. Like a saint's vision of beatitude. Like the veil of things as they seem drawn back by an unseen hand. For a second you see – and seeing the secret, are the secret. For a second there is meaning! Then the hand lets the veil fall and you are alone, lost in the fog again, and you stumble on toward nowhere, for no good reason! (*He grins wryly.*) It was a great mistake, my being born a man, I would have been much more successful as a seagull or a fish. As it is, I will always be a stranger who never feels at home, who does not really want and is not really wanted, who can never belong, who must always be a little in love with death!

COMMENTARY: *Long Day's Journey into Night* is Eugene O'Neill's most autobiographical play. In purely dramatic terms it is by far the most satisfying and successful of his plays. O'Neill's aim was to take the audience through the lived experience of a family as they pass nearly twenty-four hours in each other's close company. All their loves and hates are combined in equal measures to show an embattled family seeking accord but finding only new evidence for deep discord. Through a series of strategically divulged revelations, the sins of the past play havoc with the present.

Edmund, the sensitive youngest son of a professional actor, is an amalgam of all his mother's and his father's traits. See O'Neill's long description in the introduction above. Edmund has the gifted, silver tongue of his Papa and can set a stream of clauses and images dancing. A tongue loosened by drink allows him to 'perform' the speech as much as speak it. He should dazzle the audience with his words. He also has his mother's taste for revenge and guilt inducement. Edmund is weak and consumptive, using those physical facts to his advantage. Drinking is a danger to his health. It could kill him. So the speech and the circumstances that lead up to it imperil his life. After looking at the speech an actor may well conclude that Edmund is an extravagantly theatrical character. Indeed he is, owing much to such romantic young stage heroes as Konstantin in *The Seagull* and Shakespeare's Hamlet. This is, after all, O'Neill's portrait of himself as a young artist. So the artistry here is meant to be self-conscious. The speech is a real marathon, doubly signified by the fact that it describes an exhausting sea journey not unlike that of Coleridge's Ancient Mariner. All the characters in this play are on a long voyage home. Edmund, however, describes the trip most vividly.

Look Back in Anger
(1956) John Osborne

Act 1. The Porters' one-room flat in a large Midland town. Early evening. April, 1950s.

Jimmy Porter 'is a tall, thin young man about twenty-five, wearing a very worn tweed jacket and flannels. . . . He is a disconcerting mixture of sincerity and cheerful malice, of tenderness and freebooting cruelty; restless, importunate, full of pride, a combination which alienates the sensitive and insensitive alike. Blistering honesty, or apparent honesty, like his, makes few friends. To many he may seem sensitive to the point of vulgarity. To others, he is simply a loudmouth. To be as vehement as he is is to be almost non-committal.' He has been married to Alison for three years. He delights in taunting Alison as his domestic representative of the upper classes and hence of everything he despises. They share their dreary flat with Cliff, Jimmy's friend and partner with whom he runs a sweet stall in the local market. Jimmy's university education has only aggravated his terminal dissatisfaction and 'anger'. In this scene he indulges in one of his frequent outbursts against Alison.

JIMMY. [Don't try and patronize me. (*Turning to* CLIFF.)] She's so clumsy. I watch for her to do the same things every night. The way she jumps on the bed, as if she were stamping on someone's face, and draws the curtains back with a great clatter, in that casually destructive way of hers. It's like someone launching a battleship. Have you ever noticed how noisy women are? (*Crosses below chairs to LC.*) Have you? The way they kick the floor about, simply walking over it? Or have you watched them sitting at their dressing tables, dropping their weapons and banging down their bits of boxes and brushes and lipsticks? (*He faces her* *dressing table*.) I've watched her doing it night after night. When you see a woman in front of her bedroom mirror, you realize what a refined sort of a butcher she is. (*Turns in.*) Did you ever see some dirty old Arab, sticking his fingers into some mess of lamb fat and gristle? Well, she's just like that. Thank God they don't have many women surgeons! Those primitive hands would have your guts out in no time. Flip! Out it comes, like the powder out of its box. Flop! Back it goes, like the powder puff on the table.

[CLIFF (*grimacing cheerfully*). Ugh! Stop it!]

(*Moving upstage*.) She'd drop your guts like hair clips and fluff all over the floor. You've got to be fundamentally insensitive to be as noisy and as clumsy as that. (*He moves C, and leans against the table*.) I had a flat underneath a couple of girls once. You heard every damned thing those bastards did, all day and night. The most simple, everyday actions were a sort of assault course on your sensibilities. I used to plead with them. I even got to screaming the most ingenious obscenities I could think of, up the stairs at them. But nothing, nothing, would move them. With those two, even a simple visit to the lavatory sounded like a medieval siege. Oh, they beat me in the end – I had to go. I expect they're still at it. Or they're probably married by now, and driving some other poor devils out of their minds. Slamming their doors, stamping their high heels, banging their irons and saucepans – the eternal flaming racket of the female.

COMMENTARY: Osborne's *Look Back in Anger* was an explosive charge that changed the course of modern British drama when it was first produced at the Royal Court Theatre in 1956. Jimmy Porter, impotent with rage at all he sees, became the symbol of the disaffected, 'angry young man' of the post-war years. The play broke with the affected, polite traditions of the British stage where elegant and tidy drawing-room plays ruled the day. Osborne dared to be both profane and uncouth. British actors as varied as Kenneth Haigh, Richard Burton and Kenneth Branagh have each matched their wits with those of Jimmy Porter. Such playwrights as Harold Pinter, Simon Gray, Michael Frayn and Peter Nichols have all, in some way, followed the challenging path laid by Osborne.

Jimmy's speech is written as a diatribe, specifically against women but more generally against all social mores and habits of mind that trap both men and women. Jimmy despises routine and order. He's a born anarchist. He would probably prefer a world where spontaneous honesty, no matter how critical it might seem, was the norm and not the exception. One thing that distinguishes Jimmy from everyone else on stage, apart from his killing sarcasm, is his mobility. He moves upstage, downstage, right to left and on the diagonal. Jimmy roams around the claustrophobic flat like a caged animal, aiming accusations and questions at Alison and Cliff like scatter shot. The actor should remember that Jimmy lives in a cramped, noisy world without privacy. The speech is full of sound effects. He's a character in desperate need of space and calm. Notice, as well, all the contradictory things the playwright says about his character in the above introduction to the speech. Jimmy is a complex man with numerous facets, which he displays simultaneously. To his discredit he does like to aim his bilious venom at weaker characters like Alison.

The Maids
(1947) Jean Genet

One act. Madame's Louis-Quinze style bedroom.

*Solange Lemercier (30–35) works alongside her younger sister, Claire,
as a housemaid in Madame's house. Throughout the action they indulge
in a deadly and perverse game of role-reversing in which they
impersonate one another and their hated mistress, and then take turns
ritually killing her in mock murders. They seek revenge on Madame by
denouncing her lover, Monsieur, to the police, but this plot fails when
he is released without charge. The two sisters also feel deep jealousy,
hatred and suspicion towards one another. In this speech Solange
fantasizes that she has murdered Claire. She creates a vivid fictional
scenario for herself and addresses herself to imaginary on-stage
characters – Madame and her lover Monsieur and an Inspector.*

SOLANGE. Madame. . . . At last! Madame is dead! . . .
laid out on the linoleum . . . strangled by the dish-gloves.[1]
What? Oh, Madame may remain seated.[2] . . . Madame
may call me Mademoiselle Solange. . . . Exactly. It's
because of what I've done. Madame and Monsieur will call
me Mademoiselle Solange Lemercier. . . . Madame should
have taken off that black dress. It's grotesque. (*She imitates
MADAME's voice.*) So I'm reduced to wearing mourning
for my maid. As I left the cemetery all the servants of the
neighbourhood marched past me as if I were a member of
the family. I've so often been part of the family. Death will

---

[1] **Madame . . . dish-gloves** Solange here is referring to the murdered Claire as
'Madame.' In their role-reversal games Claire portrayed 'Madame'.
[2] **Madame may remain seated** Solange is now imagining herself addressing her real
mistress, Madame.

see the joke through to the bitter end. . . . What? Oh! Madame needn't feel sorry for me. I'm Madame's equal and I hold my head high. . . . Oh! And there are things Monsieur doesn't realize. He doesn't know that he used to obey our orders. (*She laughs.*) Ah! Ah! Monsieur was a tiny little boy. Monsieur toed the line when we threatened. No, Inspector, no. . . . I won't talk! I won't say a word. I refuse to speak about our[3] complicity in this murder. . . . The dresses? Oh, Madame could have kept them. My sister and I had our own. Those we used to put on at night, in secret. Now, I have my own dress, and I'm your equal. I wear the red garb of criminals. Monsieur's laughing at me? He's smiling at me. Monsieur thinks I'm mad. He's thinking maids should have better taste than to make gestures reserved for Madame! Monsieur really forgives me? Monsieur is the soul of kindness. He'd like to vie with me in grandeur. But I've scaled the fiercest heights. Madame now sees my loneliness – at last! Yes, I am alone. And fearsome. I might say cruel things, but I can be kind. . . . Madame will get over her fright. She'll get over it well enough. What with her flowers and perfumes and gowns and jewels and lovers. As for me, I've my sister. . . . Yes. I dare speak of these things. I do, Madame. There's nothing I won't dare. And who could silence me, who? Who would be so bold as to say to me: 'My dear child!' I've been a servant. Well and good. I've made the gestures a servant must make. I've smiled at Madame. I've bent down to make the bed, bent down to scrub the tiles, bent down to peel the vegetables, to listen at doors, to glue my eye to keyholes! But now I stand upright. And firm. I'm the strangler. Mademoiselle Solange, the one who strangled her sister! . . . Me be still? Madame is

[3] **our** Solange throughout the play speaks on behalf of herself and Claire, creating a collective self. (Notice this use again later in the speech, 'That's our business' and 'That, my child, is our darkness, ours.')

delicate, really. But I pity Madame. I pity Madame's whiteness, her satiny skin, and her little ears, and little wrists. . . . Eh? I'm the black crow. . . . Oh! Oh! I have my judges. I belong to the police. Claire? She was really very fond of Madame. . . . YOUR dresses again! And THAT white dress, THAT one, which I forbade her to put on, the one you wore the night of the Opera Ball, the night you poked fun at her, because she was sitting in the kitchen admiring a photo of Gary Cooper. . . . Madame will remember. Madame will remember her gentle irony, the maternal grace with which she took the magazine from us, and smiled. Nor will Madame forget that she called her Clarinette. Monsieur laughed until the tears rolled down his cheeks. . . . Eh? Who am I? The monstrous soul of servantdom! No, Inspector, I'll explain nothing in their presence. That's *our* business. It would be a fine thing if masters could pierce the shadows where servants live. . . . That, my child, is our darkness, ours. (*She lights a cigarette and smokes clumsily. The smoke makes her cough.*) Neither you nor anyone else will be told anything. Just tell yourselves that this time Solange has gone through with it. . . . You see her dressed in red. She is going out. (*She goes to the window, opens it, and steps out on the balcony. Facing the night, with her back to the audience, she delivers the following speech. A slight breeze makes the curtains stir.*) Going out. Descending the great stairway. Accompanied by the police. Out on your balconies to see her making her way among the shadowy penitents! It's noon. She's carrying a nine-pound torch. The hangman follows close behind. He's whispering sweet nothings in her ear. Claire! The hangman's by my side! Now take your hand off my waist. He's trying to kiss me! Let go of me! Ah! Ah! (*She laughs.*) The hangman's trifling with me. She will be led in procession by all the maids of the neighbourhood, by all the servants who accompanied Claire to her final resting place. They'll all be wearing crowns, flowers, streamers,

94

banners. They'll toll the bell. The funeral will unfold its pomp. It's beautiful, isn't it? First come the butlers, in full livery, but without silk lining. Then come the footmen, the lackeys in knee breeches and stockings. They're wearing their crowns. Then come the valets, and then the chamber-maids wearing our colours. Then the porters. And then come the delegations from heaven. And I'm leading them. The hangman's lulling me. I'm being acclaimed. I'm pale and I'm about to die . . . (*She returns to the room.*) And what flowers! They gave her such a lovely funeral, didn't they? Oh! Claire, poor little Claire! (*She bursts into tears and collapses into an armchair.*) What? (*She gets up.*) It's no use, Madame, I'm obeying the police. They're the only ones who understand me. They too belong to the world of outcasts, the world you touch only with tongs. (*Visible only to the audience,* CLAIRE, *during the last few moments, has been leaning with her elbows against the jamb of the kitchen door and listening to her sister.*) Now we are Mademoiselle Solange Lemercier, that Lemercier woman. The famous criminal. And above all, Monsieur need not be uneasy. I'm not a maid. I have a noble soul. . . . (*She shrugs her shoulders.*) No, no, not another word, my dear fellow. Ah, Madame's not forgetting what I've done for her. . . . No, no she must not forget my devotion. . . . (*Meanwhile* CLAIRE *enters through the door at the left. She is wearing the white dress.*) And in spite of my forbidding it, Madame continues to stroll about the apartment. She will please sit down . . . and listen to me . . . (*To* CLAIRE.) Claire . . . we're raving!

Translation by Bernard Frechtman

COMMENTARY: This speech, written for a female character, is included here as a challenge for a male actor. The world of Genet, an avowed homosexual, is partly one of cross-dressing and

95

transsexuality. Important productions of this modern classic have featured men in the central roles. When a man performs this speech a whole new set of associations comes into play for the audience. Illusion and reality are so fiercely pitted against one another in *The Maids* that the notion of gender bending is not at all out of place. It simply becomes one more facet of the provocative scenario.

The world of a Genet play is conceived as a macabre cabaret in which fantasy and wish-fulfilment play crucial roles. In *The Maids* (the ultimate in master/servant relationship plays) black humour, transformational characterization, quick costume changes and a rich interplay of light, colour and emotions together create a tantalizing hall of mirrors for the audience. Our tame, civilized notions about human behaviour, identity and morality are thrown into doubt. In this grotesque carnival, Genet reveals woman's immorality to woman, and man's to man. The audience is asked to see a fractured view of themselves with all their secret desires and darkest humiliations exposed in the process.

The actor is the chief vehicle in this enterprise. This is Solange's great chance to voice all the resentments, frustrations and jealousies of her subjection and submission. She is indulging in a potent fantasy as she asserts her independent identity. Solange plays many roles, many versions of herself: a sister, a maid, a lover, her Madame and a murderess. She concocts a bizarre and sometimes schizophrenic pageant of sub-plots and counterplots. The murder and funeral she describes are just further charades. The actor must convince the audience that what they are hearing and seeing while in these different guises is real. The image of the dress is used as a talisman, conjuring up alternative notions of religious purity and sullied degradation. There can be no denying that the speech is also like a surreal nightmare. The progress of the narrative journey has a rather gothic fury that should engage the performer at every turn. At all costs try to avoid a psychological or naturalistic interpretation of the speech. That will only freeze you in your tracks and reduce Genet's speculative theatrical exuberance to a single level of meaning.

Murder in the Cathedral
(1935) T. S. Eliot

Part 1. The Archbishop's Hall, Canterbury. December 2nd, 1170.

Archbishop Thomas Becket (40s) returns to his Cathedral at Canterbury after seven years in exile and against the wishes of King Henry II. Becket is all too aware that his return will provoke Henry to order his murder. These two proud men, originally close friends, fell out over the respective powers of Church and State. Four Tempters confront Becket in the Cathedral. Each of them offers him a choice of action and represents a facet of his personality – returning to 'the good times past' and his friendship with the King; becoming Chancellor and consolidating his power and position; leading a nationalist rebellion in league with the barons against the King; giving himself up to God and to inevitable martyrdom. In this speech he reflects on his options as he addresses the Chorus of Women of Canterbury.

THOMAS. Now is my way clear, now is the meaning
  plain:
Temptation shall not come in this kind again.
The last temptation is the greatest treason:
To do the right deed for the wrong reason.
The natural vigour in the venial sin
Is the way in which our lives begin.
Thirty years ago, I searched all the ways
That lead to pleasure, advancement and praise.
Delight in sense, in learning and in thought,
Music and philosophy, curiosity,
The purple bullfinch in the lilac tree,
The tiltyard skill, the strategy of chess,
Love in the garden, singing to the instrument,

Were all things equally desirable.
Ambition comes when early force is spent
And when we find no longer all things possible.
Ambition comes behind and unobservable.
Sin grows with doing good. When I imposed the King's
   law
In England, and waged war with him against Toulouse,
I beat the barons at their own game. I
Could then despise the men who thought me most
   contemptible,
The raw nobility, whose manners matched their finger-
   nails.
While I ate out of the King's dish
To become servant of God was never my wish.
Servant of God has chance of greater sin
And sorrow, than the man who serves a king.
For those who serve the greater cause may make the cause
   serve them,
Still doing right: and striving with political men
May make that cause political, not by what they do
But by what they are. I know
What yet remains to show you of my history
Will seem to most of you at best futility,
Senseless self-slaughter of a lunatic,
Arrogant passion of a fanatic.
I know that history at all times draws
The strangest consequence from remotest cause.
But for every evil, every sacrilege,
Crime, wrong, oppression and the axe's edge,
Indifference, exploitation, you, and you,
And you, must all be punished. So must you.
I shall no longer act or suffer, to the sword's end.
Now my good Angel, who God appoints
To be my guardian, hover over the swords' points.

COMMENTARY: *Murder in the Cathedral* is a verse drama about a spiritual quest. In this play T. S. Eliot hoped to restore grandeur to the modern theatre by using the tried and tested techniques of such medieval plays as *Everyman* and the more sophisticated verse drama of the sixteenth century. It was written to be performed at the Canterbury Festival in 1935 and then was produced in London's West End.

In this speech Becket confronts his own mortality and the inevitability of his martyrdom. For the most part, the speech is written in rhyming couplets with every two lines forming a complete unit of thought. Becket is explaining the motivations and choices that have determined his life. This speech is delivered in a church setting so the actor must try to create a sense of aura and scale for his audience. In a public setting Becket is confiding his most inner thoughts and secret doubts. The actor should notice that Becket presents his thoughts both as a sermon and a confession. The speech charts the journey of a soul as it takes its detours in the world before returning to God's bosom and the side of the good angels. Becket is a character literally beset by tempters and reflects on a life of temptation. The structure of the verse allows you to give it a big sound. The language combines elements of formal ancient speech and colloquial modern diction. Compare this speech with Anouilh's version of Becket (*see page 14*).

Napoli Milionaria
(1945) Eduardo de Filippo

Act 1. A large, dirty, smoke-blackened room in a Neapolitan house, 1942. Morning.

Amadeo is 'a young man in his early twenties, slim, dark-skinned, pleasant of manner and not too robust. He wears a faded, woollen, well-darned vest.' He lives at home with his parents and sisters in cramped quarters. He works for the gas company and has so far avoided being conscripted into the army. He has a volatile personality and is easily provoked. Much against his father's wishes, Amadeo and his mother run a modest black market operation from the house. He regularly clashes with his benignly moral, old-fashioned father, as well as anyone else who gets in his way. In this scene, as he is trying to get ready for work his father embarks on one of his moral sermons, observing that the coffee that Amadeo and his mother sell illegally has been stolen from 'the clinics and the hospitals and the infirmaries and the children's wards and the . . .'. Having already squabbled with his sister, Amadeo now turns on his father.

AMADEO. Give over, father. Give it a rest. Talk about getting out of your depth. You're fifteen feet under, mate, and your mouth's full of shit. You're talking a load of old cobblers. What clinics? What infirmaries? They don't get a sniff of coffee. So how can they sell it, if they haven't got none? You've got to face facts, mate. Who was it came round here the other day offering mother five kilos of coffee at seventy lire a kilo? You know perfectly well who it was. Some big, fat, bloated Fascist high-up. Course it was. And the only reason mother didn't buy it was because she didn't know who it was. For all she knew it could have been a trap –

a typical police fit-up. Course it could. We're talking about facts here. We're talking about the high-ups who should be setting a good example to poor, ignorant, starving scum like us. Good example my backside. All they are is a load of thieves and crooks. So you look at them in their smart suits and their swanky cars and you say to yourself – you know, mate, you've got the right idea. You're on top of the world, aren't you? You've got a wallet full of dosh and a great big, fat, groaning belly. And what about me? I'm dying of starvation. So what's the answer? Simple. What's good enough for you, is good enough for me. Right? Let's all steal. Right? What's yours is mine. Everyone for himself. Everyone steals. Right?

[GENNARO (*off*). Oh no. Oh no, you don't my son. As long as you live in this house you do not steal. Understand me? You never ever steal. You don't even think of stealing. You don't even mention the word.]

All right, all right, keep your wool on. I was only joking. God, can't we even crack a few measly jokes now? (*The quarrel in the street has all but finished now. He shrugs his shoulders.*) Ah, bugger the coffee. I'll get myself some breakfast.

Translation by Peter Tinniswood

COMMENTARY: Eduardo de Filippo's Neapolitan comedies are naturalistic domestic dramas rich in humour and colloquial dialogue. As an actor-playwright with his own company de Filippo was all too aware of the needs of the actor. He created roles and dialogue which invite the actor to shine in performance. All of his characters exist on an emotional plane, displaying their anxieties, frustrations and silliness while trying to maintain an existence in hard times. *Napoli Milionaria* follows the exploits of common people who set up a black market enterprise in the midst of the Second World War.

A character like Amadeo has come of age during wartime. His sense of values is non-existent as a result of sheer deprivation. This is also a world in which family values have eroded in favour of a dog-eat-dog code of survival. The smallest quarrel – here over coffee – can erupt into moral (or amoral) outrage. Amadeo sees himself as an individual not a family member. He will learn to use a system where government officials are no more than Fascist robbers. They, not his father, have set the example and he will follow. He also takes this chance to get back at his father and he is not going to let anyone interrupt him. Notice how sneering he is and how he lashes out at his father with taunting rhetorical questions.

The Night of the Iguana
(1961) Tennessee Williams

Act 3. The wide verandah of a rustic hotel in Mexico, 1940.
Summer.

*Reverend Lawrence T. Shannon (35) is an Irish American, a 'young
man who has cracked up before and is going to crack up again – perhaps
repeatedly'. He was defrocked as an Episcopalian minister for, as he
says, 'fornication and heresy'. He also has an alcohol problem. For the
past ten years he has earned his living as a tour guide in Mexico and
despite loathing the job it is his only hope. His behaviour has become
increasingly irresponsible and reckless. He has brought his current
group, from an all-female college in Texas, to a hotel run by Maxine
Faulk, a widow who has known him for many years and has a
flirtatious interest in him. After he seduces an underage girl, the leader
of the group complains to the tour company and they send another guide
to replace Shannon. As he confronts his failure in a state of frenzied
panic he runs off to 'swim to China', but he is humiliatingly dragged
back and tied up in a hammock. Hannah Jelkes, an unmarried artist
travelling with her poet grandfather, has been his only ally and she
loosens his ropes. Together they experience a spiritual one-night stand.
Here he talks to her of the iguana tied up under the verandah.*

SHANNON. [I'll get my flashlight. I'll show you] . . . It's
an iguana. I'll show you. . . . See? The iguana? At the end of
its rope? Trying to go on past the end of its goddam rope?
Like *you*! Like *me*! Like Grampa with his last poem!
[HANNAH. What is a – what – iguana?]
It's a kind of lizard – a big one, a giant one. The Mexican
kids caught it and tied it up.
[HANNAH. Why did they tie it up?]
Because that's what they do. They tie them up and fatten

103

them up and then eat them up, when they're ready for eating. They're a delicacy. Taste like white meat of chicken. At least the Mexicans think so. And also the kids, the Mexican kids, have a lot of fun with them, poking out their eyes with sticks and burning their tails with matches. You know? Fun? Like that?

[HANNAH. Mr Shannon, please go down and cut it loose!

SHANNON. I can't do that.

HANNAH. Why can't you?]

Mrs Faulk wants to eat it. I've got to please Mrs Faulk, I am at her mercy. I am at her disposal.

[HANNAH. I don't understand. I mean I don't understand how anyone could eat a big lizard.

SHANNON. Don't be so critical.] If you got hungry enough you'd eat it too. You'd be surprised what people will eat if hungry. There's a lot of hungry people still in the world. Many have died of starvation, but a lot are still living and hungry, believe you me, if you will take my word for it. Why, when I was conducting a party of – *ladies*? – yes, ladies . . . through a country that shall be nameless but in this world, we were passing by rubberneck bus along a tropical coast when we saw a great mound of . . . well, the smell was unpleasant. One of my ladies said, 'Oh, Larry, what is that?' My name being Lawrence, the most familiar ladies sometimes call me Larry. I didn't use the four-letter word for what the great mound was. I didn't think it was necessary to say it. Then she noticed, and I noticed too, a pair of very old natives of this nameless country, practically naked except for a few filthy rags, creeping and crawling about this mound of . . . and occasionally stopping to pick something out of it, and pop it into their mouths. What? Bits of undigested . . . food particles, Miss Jelkes. (*There is silence for a moment. She makes a gagging sound in her throat and rushes the length of the verandah to the wooden steps and disappears for a while,* SHANNON *continues, to himself and the moon.*) Now why did I tell her that? Because it's true? That's no reason to tell her, because it's true. Yeah. Because it's true was a good reason not to tell her. Except . . . I think I first *faced* it in that nameless country. The gradual, rapid, natural, unnatural – predestined, accidental – cracking up and going to pieces of young Mr T. Lawrence Shannon, yes, still *young* Mr T. Lawrence Shannon, by which rapid-slow process . . . his final tour of ladies through tropical countries . . . Why did I say 'tropical'? Hell! Yes! It's always been tropical countries I took ladies through. Does that, does that – huh? – signify something, I wonder? Maybe. Fast decay is a thing of hot climates, steamy, hot, wet climates, and I run back to them like a . . . Incomplete sentence. . . . Always seducing a lady or two, or three or four or five ladies in the party, but really ravaging her first by pointing out to her the – what? – horror? Yes, horrors! – of the tropical country being conducted a tour through. My . . . brain's going out now, like a failing power. . . . So I stay here, I reckon, and live off la patrona for the rest of my life. Well, she's old enough to predecease me. She could check out of here first, and I imagine that after a couple of years of having to satisfy her I might be prepared for the shock of her passing on. . . . Cruelty . . . pity. What is it? . . . Don't know, all I know is . . .

COMMENTARY: Williams' *The Night of the Iguana* shows us a group of lost characters who will do almost anything to survive. They are in flight from both civilization and themselves, taking refuge in a cheap hotel in Mexico where they experience their moment of truth. In the 1964 film version, Richard Burton was able to capture the seedy charisma that is such a key component of this central role.

Shannon is a character who, even when sober, has the gift of the gab. His Irish nature comes through in this monologue. He is a character who is used to escaping and slipping out of everyone's grasp. What he knows about life has its barbarous aspects. In a previous life as a minister he was in touch with the sacred. In his current marginal existence he is in touch with the profane. He also enjoys scaring women with provocative details. Throughout the play Shannon finds himself at the mercy of women of all ages. He's like a little boy out to reveal one slimy thing after another. So the iguana is a natural metaphor for him to draw on. By this point in the play language is failing Shannon and he can only speak in fragments that become increasingly scattered as the monologue proceeds. Shannon is in deep despair. His life is collapsing and he is hopelessly split between the inarticulate cravings of the spirit and the lure of the flesh.

Otherwise Engaged
(1975) Simon Gray

Act 2. The living-room of Hench's house in London.

Simon Hench (39) is a publisher who lives in a comfortably appointed house in London. Simon and his wife Beth have no children to interfere with their sophisticated and civilized lifestyle. Simon maintains a cool, selfish distance, remaining 'otherwise engaged' from all the emotional demands and personal problems of his friends, family and colleagues. His attempts to listen to a recording of Wagner's opera 'Parsifal' are frustrated as a series of acquaintances invade his calm, starting with his laconic student lodger, Dave and climaxing when one of his friends reveals that Beth has been having an affair. When Beth is finally alone with Simon she wants to discuss 'an important problem' and Simon responds to her with this evasively articulate speech.

SIMON. In my experience, the worst thing you can do to an important problem is discuss it. You know – (*Sitting down.*) – I really do think this whole business of non-communication is one of the more poignant fallacies of our zestfully over-explanatory age. Most of us understand as much as we need to without having to be told – except old Dave, of course, now I thought he had quite an effective system, a tribute really to the way in which even the lowest amongst us can put our education (or lack of it, in Dave's case) to serving our needs. He's done really remarkably well out of taking the metaphors of courtesy literally, as for example when he asks for a loan that is in fact a gift, and one replies, 'Of course, Dave, no trouble, pay it back when you can.' *But* this system completely collapses when he's faced with a plainly literal reply, as for example when he asks to borrow our coffee set, and he's told that it'll be lent with reluctance and one would like him to be careful with it. Weird, isn't it, he can take one's courteous metaphors literally, but he can't take one's literal literally, he translates them into metaphors for insults, and plans, I'm reasonably happy to inform you, to move out at once. So I've managed one useful thing today, after all. When we come to think of his replacement, let's narrow our moral vision slightly, and settle for a pair of respectably married and out of date homosexuals who still think they've something to hide. They'll leave us entirely alone, and we can congratulate ourselves on doing them a good turn. We'll have to raise the rent to just this side of exorbitant of course, or they'll smell something fishy, but we'll pass the money straight on to charities for the aged, unmarried mothers, that sort of thing and no one need be the wiser, what do you think?

COMMENTARY: Simon Gray's *Otherwise Engaged* is a melancholic comedy. There is a keen wit in all of Gray's dramas that harks back to the great Restoration plays of the eighteenth century. Yet the wit and parrying humour are used to disguise deep hurts and keep the central character disengaged. Gray's characters love to talk, often using language as an intellectual defence against emotion. They all indulge in destructive games of power and passion, accusation and recrimination.

Simon can be witty, cruel and selfish. He has an innate sense of his own superiority and takes a dim view of the rest of humankind. In this speech he articulates his theory of communication, practising what he preaches. He uses language like a large deflecting shield. By means of carefully crafting sentences he is able to distance and control any threatening invaders. His dextrous use of language will always protect him from any emotional involvement. Sarcasm and wit are two of his favourite devices. If he speaks loud and long enough, the real Simon won't be discovered; his own feelings will remain hidden. He talks to avoid the problem, changing the subject to avoid the main topic. Simon has no problem communicating, but he does have a problem connecting. The actor should see him as a talking head who keeps his heart well hidden.

Present Laughter

(1942) Noël Coward

Act 1. Garry Essendine's Studio in London. The furnishing is comfortable if a trifle eccentric. It is about 10.30 am.

Garry Essendine, 'Forty in December', is a famous actor in the West End and on Broadway. He is vain and witty and a notorious womanizer. In this scene a young, aspiring provincial playwright has secured an interview with Garry. He vehemently outlines his critique of the contemporary theatre, arguing that only by appearing in his plays will Garry be able to secure his place in posterity. Here Garry offers his own reaction.

GARRY. I don't give a hoot about posterity. Why should I worry about what people think of me when I'm as dead as a doornail, anyway? My worst defect is that I am apt to worry too much about what people think of me when I'm alive. But I'm not going to do that any more. I'm changing my methods and you're my first experiment. As a rule, when insufferable young beginners have the impertinence to criticize me, I dismiss the whole thing lightly because I'm embarrassed for them and consider it not quite fair game to puncture their inflated egos too sharply. But this time my highbrow young friend you're going to get it in the neck. To begin with, your play is not a play at all. It's a meaningless jumble of adolescent, pseudo intellectual poppycock. It bears no relation to the theatre or to life or to anything. And you yourself wouldn't be here at all if I hadn't been bloody fool enough to pick up the telephone when my secretary wasn't looking. Now that you are here, however, I would like to tell you this. If you wish to be a playwright you just leave the theatre of tomorrow to take care of itself. Go and get yourself a job as a butler in a repertory company if they'll have you. Learn from the ground up how plays are constructed and what is actable and what isn't. Then sit down and write at least twenty plays one after the other and if you can manage to get the twenty-first produced for a Sunday night performance you'll be damned lucky!

COMMENTARY: Noël Coward said of *Present Laughter*: 'It was written with the intention of providing me with a bravura part. It was an enormous success.' The assured ego implied in that statement was a Coward trait and accounts for the enormous success he enjoyed throughout a lengthy stage career. One can see a good deal of the man in his characters.

Garry loves to have an audience. His favourite form of conversation is the monologue. His favourite topic is himself. Ironically his tirades fail to distance people; they merely become more enamoured by his theatrical attraction. He is a character manufactured by the stage: vain, puffed-up, defined by speech. Little of the inner man is on display so the actor must concentrate here on the outward show. Garry does have one saving grace: he has an unerring eye for truth and honesty. He can spot flawed talent and a fake play a mile off. His brutal honesty is refreshing but it also sounds like a well-rehearsed script. Garry has probably given variations on this same bit of advice to hundreds of aspiring young playwrights: go out and live life and then tell us about it. Each time he says it, however, it must sound original and like freshly formed pearls of wisdom.

———————

Act 2, scene 1. Garry's studio. Midnight.

Garry is alone and wearing a dressing gown over his evening clothes. His privacy is interrupted when Joanna, a glamorous, seductive actress unexpectedly arrives. She tells Garry that she has locked herself out and finding no one else in has come to Garry's studio. He is very wary of her intentions which she admits are 'to get to know you a little better'. Garry resists her seductive ploys and finally turns on her in this speech.

GARRY. I was right about you from the first. . . . You're as predatory as hell! . . . You got the wretched Henry when he was convalescent, you've made a dead set at Morris, and now by God you're after me! Don't deny it – I can see it in your eye. You suddenly appear out of the night reeking with the lust of conquest, the whole atmosphere's quivering with it! You had your hair done this afternoon, didn't you? and your nails and probably your feet too! That's a new dress, isn't it? Those are new shoes! You've never worn those stockings before in your life! And your mind, even more expertly groomed to vanquish than your body. Every word, every phrase, every change of mood cunningly planned. Just the right amount of sex antagonism mixed with subtle flattery, just the right switch over, perfectly timed, from provocative implication to wistful diffidence. You want to know what I'm really like do you, under all the glittering veneer? Well, this is it. This is what I'm really like – fundamentally honest! When I'm driven into a corner I tell the truth, and the truth at the moment is that I know you, Joanna. I know what you're after, I can see through every trick. Go away from me! Leave me alone!

COMMENTARY: In this speech Garry gets to vent his spleen once again, but this time a 'predatory' female is his subject. The whole of his day, and now his evening has been interrupted by one person or another. Now it is midnight and Joanna's arrival must seem like the last straw. The actor must convey Garry's genuine exasperation and not just the surface of his deprecating wit. He is instantly wise to Joanna, criticizing her unsubtle approach as though she were a familiar character from a play. He's obviously seen this performance before, on and off stage. He is like a cruel theatre critic or director. Once he gets going there can be no interruptions. This is a monologue that demands style and bravura, but it will only appear hollow and mannered if you do not balance this with the genuine honesty and emotion that a character like Garry possesses.

The Price
(1968) Arthur Miller

Act 2. New York. The attic of a Manhattan brownstone on the point of demolition.

Walter Franz is 'in his mid-fifties, well barbered; hatless, in a camel's-hair coat, very healthy complexion. A look of sharp intelligence on his face.' Walter and his younger brother Victor, a policeman, meet at the house of their dead father to arrange the sale of its contents. Walter has been a successful surgeon. Victor gave up his early ambition to be a scientist to take care of their father, and he feels that Walter's success has been achieved at his expense. Over the years the two brothers have become alienated. This encounter raises memories of their childhood as they discuss the 'price' to be placed on the objects in the house. Here Walter confesses to Victor and his wife, Esther, that his successful life is not all that it seems. After a nervous breakdown and a divorce he now lives a modest and simple life.

WALTER (*with a removed self-amusement*). Oh, I owned three nursing homes. There's big money in the aged, you know. Helpless, desperate children trying to dump their parents – nothing like it. I even pulled out of the market. Fifty per cent of my time now is in City hospitals. And I tell you, I'm alive. For the first time. I do medicine, and that's it. (*Attempting an intimate grin.*) Not that I don't soak the rich occasionally, but only enough to live, really. (*It is as though this was his mission here, and he waits for* VICTOR's *comments.*)
[VICTOR. Well, that must be great.]
(*Seizing on this minute encouragement.*) Vic, I wish we could talk for weeks, there's so much I want to tell you. . . . (*It is*
114

not rolling quite the way he would wish and he must pick examples of his new feelings out of the air.) I never had friends – you probably know that. But I do now, I have good friends. (*He moves, sitting nearer* VICTOR, *his enthusiasm flowing.*) It all happens so gradually. You start out wanting to be the best, and there's no question that you do need a certain fanaticism; there's so much to know and so little time. Until you've eliminated everything extraneous – (*He smiles.*) – including people. And of course the time comes when you realize that you haven't merely been specializing in something – something has been specializing in you. You become a kind of instrument, an instrument that cuts money out of people, or fame out of the world. And it finally makes you stupid. Power can do that. You get to think that because you can frighten people they love you. Even that you love them. – And the whole thing comes down to fear. One night I found myself in the middle of my living room, dead drunk with a knife in my hand, getting ready to kill my wife.
[ESTHER. Good Lord!]
Oh ya – and I nearly made it too! (*He laughs.*) But there's one virtue in going nuts – provided you survive, of course. You get to see the terror – not the screaming kind, but the slow, daily fear you call ambition, and cautiousness, and piling up the money. And really, what I wanted to tell you for some time now – is that you helped me to understand that in myself.

COMMENTARY: Miller's *The Price* is a solid and sincere examination of sibling rivalry and human exploitation. It explores the 'price' to be placed on love. As the two brothers confront one another they are also forced to confront themselves and work together. The tightly structured drama is full of confessions, revelations and recriminations. It asks key questions about the demands and sacrifices of family relationships and the values and virtues of professional and material success. In many ways the play revives the famous attic scene in Miller's earlier play *Death of a Salesman* between Willy Loman's sons, Happy and Biff. *The Price*, like all of Miller's dramas, is a traditional well-made play full of well-crafted dialogue.

Walter's well-kept appearance hides a few unattractive features. The pressures of wife, profession and life all tumble forth in this concentrated speech. Walter certainly hasn't planned what he is going to say. The actor must show Walter thinking on the spot, improvising his confession. You must decide how much he is in control of what he is saying and how much he is responding to a sudden sense of release. Once he launches into his narrative, he just keeps embellishing it with more details and revelations. Notice that he is eager for Victor's response, and especially his encouragement. Victor does not respond in quite the way that Walter seems to expect and Miller helps the actor by indicating the unsettling effect this has on Walter. His speech is riddled with a deep sense of guilt and sadness, but Walter is not seeking pity. He wants an audience for his confession; the very act of speaking gives him relief. Within the space of a few minutes Walter reveals all to his brother. As you go through the speech notice all the topics Walter manages to cover, culminating in the unexpected revelation of a death wish. All of a sudden the impeccable Walter is no longer the man he once seemed to be. In typical Miller fashion, the character reveals all at a crucial point in the drama.

Pygmalion
(1912) Bernard Shaw

Act 5. Mrs Higgins' drawing-room.

Henry Higgins (40 'or thereabouts') is a professor of phonetics and a confirmed bachelor. He observes Eliza Doolittle, a Cockney flower-girl, plying her trade in Covent Garden. He wagers with Colonel Pickering (an expert in Indian languages) that he can transform Eliza into a 'lady'. Higgins rigorously coaches her in the arts of speech and etiquette. At a society ball Eliza successfully passes herself off as a duchess and Higgins gleefully wins his wager with Colonel Pickering. During Higgins' 'experiment' she is a guest in his house but he never once thinks of the effect the radical transformation or close contact will have on Eliza; he treats her merely as an object. After her triumph at the ball Higgins offers her no praise but merely asks her to find his slippers. It is then that Eliza realizes that she means nothing to Higgins and so she walks out on him, seeking refuge at his mother's house. He comes in pursuit of her and admits that he has 'grown accustomed' to her face. When she accuses him of not 'caring' for her and 'sneering', Higgins responds with this speech.

HIGGINS. I have never sneered in my life. Sneering doesnt become either the human face or the human soul. I am expressing my righteous contempt for Commercialism. I dont and wont trade in affection. You call me a brute because you couldnt put a claim on me by fetching my slippers and finding my spectacles. You were a fool: I think a woman fetching a man's slippers is a disgusting sight: did I ever fetch your slippers? I think a good deal more of you for throwing them in my face. No use slaving for me and then saying you want to be cared for: who cares for a slave? If you come back, come back for the sake of good fellowship; for youll get nothing else. Youve had a thousand times as much out of me as I have out of you; and if you dare to set up your little dog's tricks of fetching and carrying slippers against my creation of a Duchess Eliza, I'll slam the door in your silly face.

[LIZA. What did you do it for if you didnt care for me?

HIGGINS (*heartily*). Why, because it was my job.

LIZA. You never thought of the trouble it would make for me.]

Would the world ever have been made if its maker had been afraid of making trouble? Making life means making trouble. Theres only one way of escaping trouble; and thats killing things. Cowards, you notice, are always shrieking to have troublesome people killed.

[LIZA. I'm no preacher: I dont notice things like that. I notice that you dont notice me.]

(*Jumping up and walking about intolerably*.) Eliza: youre an idiot. I waste the treasures of my Miltonic mind by spreading them before you. Once for all, understand that I go my way and do my work without caring twopence what happens to either of us. I am not intimidated, like your father and your stepmother. So you can come back or go to the devil: which you please.

COMMENTARY: Shaw's *Pygmalion* updates the classical myth of Pygmalion and Galatea – the story of an artist who brings a statue to life. The play itself comes to life most passionately and theatrically when it debates and tests ideas about human communication. Higgins transforms Eliza from a vital, roughly formed individual into a petrified model of perfect grace, reversing the process of his mythical counterpart. When Eliza frees herself from Higgins' tutelage her transformation is complete. Then she becomes a 'new' woman with her own freedom and independence.

Henry Higgins is an odd man and very much a loner. In this

revealing speech he speaks not of love but of friendship. He postulates what that can mean to two people on equal footing. The actor must always remember that Higgins has a passion for work and knowledge but very little understanding of people. He can talk of treating Eliza as an equal because he believes he has created her in his own image and likeness. She's a projection of his ego. In being brutally frank with her he is just being candid with himself. The actor must decide for himself whether Higgins is a giving man or simply a selfish one. Has he liberated Eliza or simply imprisoned her in a different sort of casing? Notice throughout the exchange that Henry Higgins is a character of enormous intellect, compared with Eliza Doolittle who is all instinct. Higgins' chief flaw is that he has never seen himself through the eyes of other people. If he did he would most probably have caught himself sneering at them.

Shaw, in his usual fashion, appraised his own characters best of all: he describes Higgins as 'of the energetic, scientific type, heartily, even violently interested in everything that can be studied as a scientific subject, and careless about himself and other people, including their feelings. He is, in fact, but for his years and size, rather like a very impetuous baby "taking notice" eagerly and loudly, and requiring almost as much watching to keep him out of intended mischief. His manner varies from genial bullying when he is in a good humour to stormy petulance when anything goes wrong; but he is so entirely frank and void of malice that he remains likeable even in his least reasonable moments.'

The Resistible Rise of Arturo Ui
(1941) Bertolt Brecht

Scene 7. Offices of the Cauliflower Trust. Chicago in the 1930s.

Arturo Ui (30s) is a Chicago gangster who bears a striking resemblance to both Richard III and Adolf Hitler. He starts off as a small time crook with big time ambitions. He sets up a ruthless protection racket to take advantage of the tottering Cauliflower Trust that supplies vegetables to the city's grocers. His ascent to power is quick and brutal. In this scene he addresses a group of vegetable dealers, outlining some of the virtues of his 'protection' scheme.

UI.   In short
Chaos is rampant. Because if everybody
Can do exactly what he pleases, if
Dog can eat dog without a second thought
I call it chaos. Look. Suppose I'm sitting
Peacefully in my vegetable store
For instance, or driving my cauliflower truck
And someone comes barging not so peacefully
Into my store: 'Hands up!' Or with his gun
Punctures my tyres. Under such conditions
Peace is unthinkable. But once I know
The score, once I recognize that men are not
Innocent lambs, then I've got to find a way
To stop these men from smashing up my shop and
Making me, when it suits them, put 'em up
And keep 'em up, when I could use my hands
For better things, for instance, counting pickles.
For such is man. He'll never put aside

120

His hardware of his own free will, say
For love of virtue, or to earn the praises
Of certain silver tongues at city hall.
If I don't shoot, the other fellow will.
That's logic. Okay. And maybe now you'll ask:
What's to be done? I'll tell you. But first get
This straight: What you've been doing so far is
Disastrous: Sitting idly at your counters
Hoping that everything will be all right
And meanwhile disunited, bickering
Among yourselves, instead of mustering
A strong defence force that would shield you from
The gangsters' depredations. No, I say
This can't go on. The first thing that's needed
Is unity. The second is sacrifices.
What sacrifices? you may ask. Are we
To part with thirty cents on every dollar
For mere protection? No, nothing doing.
Our money is too precious. If protection
Were free of charge, then yes, we'd be all for it.
Well, my dear vegetable dealers, things
Are not so simple. Only death is free:
Everything else costs money. And that includes
Protection, peace and quiet. Life is like
That, and because it never will be any different
The gentlemen and I (there are more outside)
Have resolved to offer you protection.
GIVOLA *and* ROMA *applaud.*

But

To show you that we mean to operate
On solid business principles, we've asked
Our partner, Mr Clark here, the wholesaler
Whom you all know, to come here and address you.

Translation by Ralph Manheim

COMMENTARY: Brecht's *Arturo Ui* is an entertaining parable play that depicts the rise of a grotesque Hitler-like gangster. Brecht termed the play a 'historical farce'. It tells the story of an idiot dictator who is idiotically given power. Brecht created a brilliant Shakespearian parody in verse styled on a Hollywood gangster movie. Such diverse character actors as Leonard Rossiter, Nicol Williamson, Antony Sher and John Turturro have played Arturo Ui. The role, written in blank verse, requires bravura acting and the timing of a stand-up comedian. The improbability of gangsters speaking in iambic pentameter verse gives the play a great comic power in performance.

Brecht's Ui, like Shakespeare's Richard III, is a charismatic personality. Ui uses the language and menace of the thug. The inflection of the lines gives them an awkward authority. Earlier in the play Ui has taken diction lessons from a has-been Shakespearian actor; imagine the effect this might have had on him. Notice the threatening quality of his precise rhythm and grammar. The speech is addressed directly to the audience and swings between intimidation and persuasion. The actor can explore the various tones and postures Ui would adopt, glowering, prowling and cajoling his listeners. As always, he is surrounded by his loyal henchmen, Givola and Roma; you might find a way to convey their presence. Ui is a comic monster full of neurotic twitches and childish rage. As much Charlie Chaplin as Adolf Hitler.

Rhinoceros
(1960) Eugène Ionesco

Act 3. The living-room in Berenger's small apartment.

Berenger (30s) lives in a small French town where one by one the town's inhabitants find themselves being transformed into rhinoceroses, each of them eagerly capitulating to the inevitable. Berenger, always the outsider and brave individualist, is the only one to defy the mass hysteria and maintain the integrity of his own human identity. In this scene his fiancée, Daisy, has just left him to join the herd.

BERENGER (*looking at himself in the mirror*). Men aren't so bad-looking, you know. And I'm not a particularly handsome specimen! Believe me, Daisy! (*He turns round.*) Daisy! Daisy! Where are you, Daisy? You can't do that to me! (*He darts to the door.*) Daisy! (*He gets to the landing and leans over the banister.*) Daisy! Come back! Come back, my dear! You haven't even had your lunch. Daisy, don't leave me alone! Remember your promise! Daisy! Daisy! (*He stops calling, makes a despairing gesture, and comes back into the room.*) Well, it was obvious we weren't getting along together. The home was broken up. It just wasn't working out. But she shouldn't have left like that with no explanation. (*He looks all around.*) She didn't even leave a message. That's no way to behave. Now I'm all on my own. (*He locks the door carefully, but angrily.*) But they won't get me. (*He carefully closes the windows.*) You won't get me! (*He addresses all the rhinoceros heads.*) I'm not joining you; I don't understand you! I'm staying as I am. I'm a human being. A human being. (*He sits in the armchair.*) It's an impossible situation.

It's my fault she's gone. I meant everything to her. What'll become of her? That's one more person on my conscience. I can easily picture the worst, because the worst can easily happen. Poor little thing left all alone in this world of monsters! Nobody can help me find her, nobody, because there's nobody left. (*Fresh trumpetings, hectic racings, clouds of dust.*) I can't bear the sound of them any longer, I'm going to put cotton wool in my ears. (*He does so, and talks to himself in the mirror.*) The only solution is to convince them – but convince them of what? Are the changes reversible, that's the point? Are they reversible? It would be a labour of Hercules, far beyond me. In any case, to convince them you'd have to talk to them. And to talk to them I'd have to learn their language. Or they'd have to learn mine. But what language do I speak? What is my language? Am I talking French? Yes, it must be French. But what is French? I can call it French if I want, and nobody can say it isn't – I'm the only one who speaks it. What am I saying? Do I understand what I'm saying? Do I? (*He crosses to the middle of the room.*) And what if it's true what Daisy said, and they're the ones in the right? (*He turns back to the mirror.*) A man's not ugly to look at, not ugly at all! (*He examines himself, passing his hand over his face.*) What a funny-looking thing! What do I look like? What? (*He darts to a cupboard, takes out some photographs which he examines.*) Photographs! Who are all these people? Is it Mr Papillon – or is it Daisy? And is that Botard or Dudard or Jean? Or is it me? (*He rushes to the cupboard again and takes out two or three pictures.*) Now I recognize me: that's me, that's me! (*He hangs the pictures on the back wall, beside the rhinoceros heads.*) That's me, that's me! (*When he hangs the pictures one sees that they are of an old man, a huge woman, and another man. The ugliness of these pictures is in contrast to the rhinoceros heads which have become very beautiful.* BERENGER *steps back to contemplate the pictures.*) I'm not good-looking, I'm not good-looking. (*He takes down the pictures, throws them furiously to the ground, and goes over to the mirror.*) They're the good-looking ones. I was wrong! Oh, how I wish I was like them! I haven't got any horns, more's the pity! A smooth brow looks so ugly. I need one or two horns to give my sagging face a lift. Perhaps one will grow and I needn't be ashamed any more – then I could go and join them. But it will never grow! (*He looks at the palms of his hands.*) My hands are so limp – oh, why won't they get rough! (*He takes his coat off, undoes his shirt to look at his chest in the mirror.*) My skin is so slack. I can't stand this white, hairy body. Oh I'd love to have a hard skin in that wonderful dull green colour – a skin that looks decent naked without any hair on it, like theirs! (*He listens to the trumpetings.*) Their song is charming – a bit raucous perhaps, but it does have charm! I wish I could do it! (*He tries to imitate them.*) Ahh, Ahh, Brr! No, that's not it! Try again, louder! Ahh, Ahh, Brr! No, that's not it, it's too feeble, it's got no drive behind it. I'm not trumpeting at all; I'm just howling. Ahh, Ahh, Brr! There's a big difference between howling and trumpeting. I've only myself to blame; I should have gone with them while there was still time. Now it's too late! Now I'm a monster, just a monster. Now I'll never become a rhinoceros, never, never! I've gone past changing. I want to, I really do, but I can't, I just can't. I can't stand the sight of me. I'm too ashamed! (*He turns his back on the mirror.*) I'm so ugly! People who try to hang on to their individuality always come to a bad end! (*He suddenly snaps out of it.*) Oh well, too bad! I'll take on the whole of them! I'll put up a fight against the lot of them, the whole lot of them! I'm the last man left, and I'm staying that way until the end. I'm not capitulating!

Translation by Derek Prouse

COMMENTARY: In *Rhinoceros*, Ionesco shows how ideologies can corrupt and dehumanize individuals. This beast fable with its elements of whimsy and absurdist comedy has a clear political message, warning against the dangers of blind uniformity however ridiculous. The town's inhabitants catch 'rhinoceritis'; it is the disease of conformity. Berenger is the only one who remains immune by retaining his humanity and individuality. Although he starts as an average man he ends the play by taking on the consummate role as the last representative of mankind. Such actors as Laurence Olivier, Jean-Louis Barrault and Zero Mostel have taken on the role of Berenger.

In this monologue Berenger goes through a whole range of emotions. He begins in resignation, becomes frantic and ends in quiet triumph. He is aware that time is running out. One by one he has seen everyone around him turning into beasts. He has become increasingly isolated, observing the inexorable victory of the herd instinct. Every thought that enters Berenger's head in this state of confusion is delivered to the audience. This long monologue requires careful pacing. The actor has to convey Berenger's growing panic as he confronts the fact that he is the last human being; there is no one else left to help him define himself. He has to keep talking to reassure himself that he is human, asserting and reasserting his identity. The actor must find a way to present Berenger's sudden transition as he tries desperately to transform himself into a rhinoceros. Few modern monologues provide an actor with such an opportunity to express so much range on-stage. The actor should relish each of the physical challenges. It is a speech which makes you grow and grow, ending on a note of triumphant defiance.

Rosencrantz and Guildenstern are Dead
(1966) Tom Stoppard

Act 1. A place without any visible character.

Guildenstern (20–30) is a courtier at an unnamed Elizabethan court. He and his companion, Rosencrantz, seem to have no apparent function. As the play opens they are whiling away the time betting on the toss of a coin. They have been at this for quite some time. Rosencrantz is on a winning streak. 'Guildenstern is well alive to the oddity of it. He is not worried about the money, but he is worried by the implications; aware but not going to panic about it – his character note.' Once they finally stop playing, Guildenstern ruminates on the nature of probability. When Rosencrantz asks him what he wants to do next, this is his reply.

GUILDENSTERN. I have no desires. None. (*He stops pacing dead.*) There was a messenger . . . that's right. We were sent for. (*He wheels at* ROS *and raps out –*) Syllogism the second: one, probability is a factor which operates within natural forces. Two, probability is not operating as a factor. Three, we are now within un-, sub- or supernatural forces. Discuss. (ROS *is suitably startled – Acidly.*) Not too heatedly. [ROS. I'm sorry I – What's the matter with you?] The scientific approach to the examination of phenomena is a defence against the pure emotion of fear. Keep tight hold and continue while there's time. Now – counter to the previous syllogism: tricky one, follow me carefully, it may prove a comfort. If we postulate, and we just have, that within un-, sub- or supernatural forces *the probability is* that the law of probability will not operate as a factor, then we must accept that the probability of the *first* part will not operate as a factor, in which case the law of probability *will* operate as a factor within un-, sub- or supernatural forces. And since it obviously hasn't been doing so, we can take it that we are not held within un-, sub- or supernatural forces after all; in all probability, that is. Which is a great relief to me personally. (*Small pause.*) Which is all very well, except that – (*He continues with tight hysteria, under control.*) We have been spinning coins together since I don't know when, and in all that time (if it *is* all that time) I don't suppose either of us was more than a couple of gold pieces up or down. I hope that doesn't sound surprising because its very unsurprising-ness is something I am trying to keep hold of. The equanimity of your average tosser of coins depends upon the law, or rather a tendency, or let us say a probability, or at any rate a mathematically calculable chance, which ensures that he will not upset himself by losing too much nor upset his opponent by winning too often. This made for a kind of harmony and a kind of confidence. It related the fortuitous and the ordained into a reassuring union which we recog-nized as nature. The sun came up about as often as it went down, in the long run, and a coin showed heads about as often as it showed tails. Then a messenger arrived. We had been sent for. Nothing else happened. Ninety-two coins spun consecutively have come down heads ninety-two consecutive times . . . and for the last three minutes on the wind of a windless day I have heard the sound of drums and flute. . . .

COMMENTARY: Tom Stoppard's dazzling *Rosencrantz and Guildenstern are Dead* features the two most marginal characters in Shakespeare's *Hamlet* and makes them the stars of this drama. The characters are barely distinguishable from one another. The play presents a witty meditation on the futility of life as Rosencrantz and Guildenstern try to interpret their existence, seeking the answers to certain imponderable questions. We come into the world for what purpose? Does what happen to us depend on the toss of a coin? They wait, like Beckett's two tramps in *Waiting for Godot*, for a revelation which never comes. Not even the space in which they are acting has definition.

Guildenstern is the perennial student. His understanding of the world comes from books and essays rather than from direct experience. His language, always complex and couched in the codes of philosophical discourse, shows a keen mind at work attempting to unravel life's mysterious tangles. But no matter how hard he tries to confront the problem all he has available to him is useless verbiage. The actor must share Guildenstern's relish for logic and language and find a way to make perfect sense of each of his idiosyncratic arguments. The audience must be seduced by his wordplay not bored by it. As Guildenstern progresses through the speech notice that he continues 'with tight hysteria, under control'. Stoppard skilfully constructs a very physical set of circumstances that mirror the intellectual conundrum: like characters out of a play by Pirandello, Guildenstern and Rosencrantz have been given all the lines but none of the plot. The cruel joke is that death awaits them and then comes as a complete surprise. The audience has advance knowledge of this fact but not the characters themselves. As they flip around coins and ideas, the inevitability of the mortal coil enmeshes them in its grip.

The Rules of the Game

(1919) Luigi Pirandello

Act 1. The smartly furnished drawing-room of Silia Gala's flat in an Italian town. 1919. Evening.

Leone Gala (30s–40s) is separated from his wife Silia. Although she has taken a lover, Guido Venanzi, Leone still exerts a powerful influence over her. Leone visits her but he only 'comes as far as the front door and sends the maid up to ask if I have any message for him'. This evening Silia provocatively invites Leone to come up. She runs out of the room, abandoning the embarrassed Guido to deal with Leone on his own. Leone proceeds to run metaphorical rings around Guido, explaining his philosophy of life. Both Leone and Guido are fully aware that Silia is eavesdropping on their conversation. Here Leone coolly discusses the limitations of Silia's character.

LEONE. That's a great misfortune for me, my dear Venanzi. She was a wonderful school of experience. I've come to miss her. She is full of unhappiness because she's full of life. Not one life only, many. But there isn't one of them that will ever give her an anchor. There's no salvation for her. (*Pointedly.*) And so there's no peace . . . either for her, or with her. (GUIDO, *absorbed in thought, unconsciously nods too, with a sad expression on his face.*) You agree?
[GUIDO (*thoughtfully*). Yes . . . it's perfectly true.]
You're probably unaware of all the riches there are in her . . . qualities of mind and spirit you would never believe to be hers – because you know only one facet of her character, from which you have built up your idea of what is for you and always will be, the real and only Silia. You wouldn't think it possible, for example, for Silia to go about her

130

housework some morning carefree, relaxed, happily singing or humming to herself. But she does, you know. I used to hear her sometimes, going from room to room singing in a sweet little quavering voice, like a child's. A different woman, I'm not saying that just for the sake of saying it. Really a different woman – without knowing it! For a few moments when she is out of herself, she is just a child, singing. And if you could see how she sits sometimes, absorbed, gazing into space; a distant, living glow reflected in her eyes, and unconsciously smoothing her hair with idly straying fingers. Who is she then? Not the Silia you know – another Silia, a Silia that can't live because she is unknown to herself, since no one has ever said to her 'I love you when you are like that; that's the way I want you always to be.' If you told her that she'd ask you, 'How do you want me to be?' You would reply 'As you were just now.' Then she would turn to you, 'What was I like,' she would say, 'what was I doing?' 'You were singing.' 'I was singing?' 'Yes, and you were smoothing your hair like this.' She would not know it. She would tell you it wasn't true. She positively would not recognize herself in your picture of her as you had just seen her – if you *could* see her like that, for you always see only one side of her! How sad it is, Guido! Here's a sweet, gracious potentiality of a life she might have – and she hasn't got it! (*A sad pause. In the silence, the ormolu clock strikes eleven.*) Ah, eleven o'clock. Say goodnight to her from me.

Translation by Robert Rietty & Noel Cregeen

131

pure reason and Silia of pure instinct. The play is a farce of despair.

Leone is intelligent, suave and agreeable. There is another side to him that lies just below the surface of the dialogue that is insidious, vengeful and deeply hurt. Although he admits that he willingly agreed to their mutual separation, he still suffers the loss of his wife. If he cannot have her no other man will. To defend himself from emotion and pain Leone plays life as a manipulative intellectual game entirely devoid of sentiment. He pursues this game by the rules and is the master of one-upmanship. His strategy in this speech is to sow doubts about Silia in the mind of the weaker Guido. In essence he is playing cunning mind games with Guido. Leone's version of Silia is not the passionate, flirtatious and strong-willed one that Guido thinks he knows. Notice how he insinuates that he alone knows the real Silia. The actor must decide how much of this speech is being presented for Silia's benefit (she is watching and listening), and what Leone hopes she will make of it. By the end of his summary Leone has corrupted Guido's sense of Silia.

The Ruling Class
(1968) Peter Barnes

Act 1, scene 4. The large, seventeenth-century drawing room of Gurney Manor.

Jack Gurney (late 20s–30) is a classified paranoid schizophrenic. When Jack experienced a revelation, in the unusual location of the urinal at West Acton Station, that he was Jesus Christ (J. C.) his family had him committed to a private mental clinic where he has been living for the past seven years. His delusion has however resisted all treatment. When his father, the eccentric 13th Earl of Gurney dies, Jack returns to Gurney Manor for the reading of his father's will. Much to the horror of the rest of his assembled family Jack inherits the title and the considerable estate, becoming the 14th Earl. He wears the habit of 'a Franciscan monk of the Capuchi Order. His habit is a coarse, brown tunic, cord, girdle, pointed cowl, bare feet in sandals. Tall and ascetic, the Earl has a sensitive face, fair beard and a magnetic personality.' In this monologue he reveals the extent of his delusion.

EARL OF GURNEY. QED, if I saw a man eating grass I'd say he was hungry. They'd have him certified. They claim snow is only precipitation and not candied dew, and the single heart-beat only the contraction and dilation of the central organ of the vascular system. *Whroom. (He makes a circular motion with his right hand.)* I'm always thinking so fast. Could a rooster forget he was a rooster and lay an egg? *Whroom.* Space and time only exist within the walls of my brain. What I'm trying to say is, if the words sound queer or funny to your ear, a little bit jumbled and jivy, sing mares eat oats and does eat oats and little lambs eat ivy. Ivy? Who's Ivy? . . . I . . . I am that Lord Jesus come again in my body

133

to save the sick, the troubled, the ignorant. I am He that liveth and behold I am alive for everyone. (*Opens his arms mimicking American nightclub entertainer Ted Lewis.*) Is everybody happy? Now hear this, I come to proclaim the New Dispensation. The Gospel Dispensation promised only salvation for the soul, my new Dispensation of Love gives it to the *body* as well. J. Christ Mark I suffered to redeem the spirit and left the body separated from God, so Satan found a place in man, and formed in him a false consciousness, a false love, a love of self. EXPLODE only FEEL, LOVE, and sin no more. Most everything you see, touch and FEEL glorifies my love. (*Mimes putting on a hat.*) The top hat is my mitre and the walking sick my rod. (*Twirls imaginary stick.*) I'm sorry. I really must apologize. Once I get started I find it damnable difficult to stop. They diagnose it as arbitrary discharge from the speech centre. Diarrhoea of the mouth. Nobody else gets much of a look-in.

COMMENTARY: Peter Barnes' gift as a dramatist is to take us inside the world and mind of the English eccentric. He lets the ruling class damn itself through its own strange codes of behaviour that should seem insane. His plays are unsettling and owe little to any type of dramatic convention. Part of their pleasure comes from their seemingly improvised freedom. Yet a play like *The Ruling Class*, which seems at first glance an anarchic and chaotic work, resolves itself in complete coherence when performed on-stage. Peter O'Toole has given one of his greatest performances in the central role.

Jack Gurney's delusion of divinity and religious fervour have fast overtaken him. What appears absolutely rational to him merely seems irrational to everyone else. The actor must make Jack's sense of his own sanity paramount, if you play him as merely insane the speech will be reduced to an incoherent ramble. You must fascinate your audience with the unique and vivid logic of his lunacy. His savage wit and energy are mesmerizing. Even he can barely keep up with himself. In order to do this speech justice try to balance the demonic lunacy with a measure of saintly vision. To keep up with the speech the actor must be willing to jump from line to line and thought to thought and word to word with great facility. Notice how rapidly he shifts voice and persona. Gurney speaks about things Divine but in the manner of a seaside barker or vaudeville comedian.

Sexual Perversity in Chicago
(1974) David Mamet

One act. A singles bar in Chicago. One summer.

Bernard Litko (Bernie) is an 'urban male in his late twenties'. He has just entered a singles bar and moves over to join Joan who is sitting alone. Here adopting an invented persona he begins to chat her up.

BERNIE. So here I am. I'm just in town for a one-day layover and I happen to find myself in this bar. So, so far so good. What am I going to do? I could lounge alone and lonely and stare into my drink, or I could take the bull by the horns and make an effort to enjoy myself . . .
[JOAN. Are you making this up?]
So hold on. So I see you seated at this table and I say to myself, 'Doug McKenzie, there is a young woman,' I say to myself, 'What is she doing here?', and I think she is here for the same reasons as I. To enjoy herself, and perhaps, to meet provocative people. (*Pause.*) I'm a meteorologist for TWA. It's an incredibly interesting, but lonely job . . . Stuck in the cockpit of some jumbo jet hours at a time . . . nothing to look at but charts . . . What are you drinking?
[JOAN. Scotch on the rocks?]
You're a scotch drinker, huh?
[JOAN. Yes.]
Well, what the hell, you're drinking scotch. But I say 'Why pigeonhole ourselves?' A person makes an effort to enjoy himself, why pin a label on it, huh? This is life. You learn a lot about life working for the airlines. Because you're constantly in touch, you know with what?, with the idea of
136

Death. (*Pause.*) Not that I'm a fan of morbidness, and so on. I mean what are you doing here? You're by yourself, I can see that. So what do you come here for? To what? To meet interesting new people or not. (*Pause.*) What else is there? . . . All kidding aside . . . lookit, I'm a fucking professional, huh? My life is a bunch of having to make split-second decisions. Life or death fucking decisions. So that's what it is, so okay. I work hard, I play hard. Comes I got a day off I wanna relax a bit . . . wander – quite by accident – into this bar. I have a drink or two . . . perhaps a drop too much. Perhaps I get *too* loose (it's been known to happen.) So what do I see? A nice young woman sitting by herself. . . .

The beach. One summer.

Bernie and his friend Dan Shapiro are 'watching the action' on the beach.

BERNIE. Now look over there to illustrate my point.
[DANNY. The broad?]
Right. Nice legs, eh?
[DANNY. Yup.]
Very acceptable old ass . . .
[DANNY. Nice, firm.]
Flat belly, beautiful pair of tits.
[DANNY. No question.]
Now *she* is fine. (*Pause.*)
[DANNY. Right.]
But now look over *there*. The broad with the dumpy legs and the fat whatdayacallit.
[DANNY. Stomach.]

137

Her legs are for shit, her stomach is dumpy, her tits don't say anything for her, and her muscle tone is not good.
[DANNY. Right.]
Now she is *not* a good-looking girl. (*Pause.*) In fact she is something of a pig. (*Pause.*) You see? That's all it takes to make the difference between a knockout looking broad, and a nothing looking broad who doesn't look like anything. (*Pause.*) You see my point?
[DANNY. . . . yeah?]
Makes all the fucking difference in the world. (*Pause.*) Coming out here on the beach. Lying all over the beach, flaunting their bodies . . . I mean who the fuck do they think they are all of a sudden, coming out here and just flaunting their bodies all over? (*Pause.*) I mean, what are you supposed to think? I come to the beach with a friend to get some sun and watch the action and . . . I mean a fellow comes to the beach to sit out in the fucking sun, am I wrong? . . . I mean we're talking about recreational fucking space, huh? . . . huh? (*Pause.*) What the fuck am I talking about?

COMMENTARY: David Mamet's *Sexual Perversity in Chicago* captures in comic vignettes the dating and mating habits of urban males and females. The play chronicles the relationships and sexual encounters of two young men and two young women over the course of a summer. Mamet excels at creating carefully observed, highly idiomatic contemporary dialogue.

Bernie is one of those guys who thinks he is a master of the pick-up line: a smooth-talking guy irresistible to women. He can slip into a new persona as smoothly as into a new jacket. He actually works in an office but is pretending to be a meteorologist called 'Doug' and the actor must decide why he puts on this act. He has something of the lounge lizard about him, probably from too many nights spent in dimly lit bars. On a good night Bernie probably thinks of himself as a cool, stand-up comic. Words and phrases come to him easily. The pauses and ellipses in the speech do not indicate hesitation but might be used like timing devices. He is performing as 'Doug' for Joan and the actor must always be aware of her presence and reactions. He must have done this number many times before, and most likely Joan is wise to his game. This is a slick act as Bernie tries simultaneously to impress and seduce. He likes to detonate a line, and give it a little fizz. Notice, how at the end of the first speech he brings the monologue back to its starting point ready to start the assault once again. On the beach Bernie's lust is like a directional device. He literally scans the beach like a radar dish attracted by female flesh, judging what he sees. The actor must create the feel of the beachscape and a lazy sunny afternoon for the audience. Bernie runs at the mouth hardly giving Danny a chance to get a word in. Notice how he uses obscenities as a form of rhythmic punctuation. His praise of the female form quickly degenerates into a fragmentary rant. By the end even he doesn't seem to know what he's talking about. His usual facility with words suffers a kind of sunstroke.

Spring Awakening
(1892) Frank Wedekind

Act 2, scene 7. A path near the river in a provincial German town in the 1890s.

Moritz Stiefel (14) is a schoolboy in a repressive and conservative town. He is distracted from his schoolwork by his growing curiosity about the nature of sex and death. He becomes increasingly obsessed, staying up at night to read as much as he can. The restrictions and limitations of his life feed his growing frustration. When he fails his exams he reaches a point of desperation. He writes to the mother of his best friend, Melchior, threatening to kill himself unless she gives him money to escape to America. She writes refusing him. Alone in this scene he vents all his resentments and suicidal anger.

MORITZ. The sooner the better. I don't belong here. Let them kick each other to bits. I'll shut the door behind me and walk away into freedom. Why should I let them push me about? I didn't force myself on them. Why should I force myself on them now? I haven't got a contract with God. Look at it from any angle you like, they forced me. I don't blame my parents. Still, they were old enough to know what they were doing. I was a baby when I came in the world – or I'd have had enough sense to come as someone else!

I'd have to be off my head: someone gives me a mad dog, and when he won't take his mad dog back *I* play the gentleman and . . .

I'd have to be off my head!

You're born by pure chance and after mature reconsideration you mustn't. . . ? I could die laughing! At least the weather cares. It looked like rain all day and now it's cleared.

The strange stillness everywhere. Nothing harsh or loud. The whole world like a fine cobweb. Everything so calm and still. The landscape is a beautiful lullaby. 'Sleep, little prince, go to sleep.' Fräulein Hectorina's song. A pity she holds her elbows awkwardly! The last time I danced it was the feast of St Cecilia. Hectorina only dances with young toffs. Her dress was cut so low at the back and the front. Down to the hips at the back, and in the front down to – you mustn't think about it. She couldn't have had a bodice on . . . That might keep me here. More out of curiosity. It must be a strange sensation – like being dragged over maelstroms. I won't tell anyone. I've come back half-cocked. I'll behave as if I've done everything. It's shameful to have been a man and not known the most human thing. You come from *Egypt*, dear sir, and you've never seen the pyramids?

I don't want to cry anymore. Or think about my funeral. Melchior will lay a wreath on my coffin. Reverend Baldbelly will console my parents. The Head will cite examples from history. I don't suppose I'll get a tombstone. I'd have liked a snow-white marble urn on a black syenite column – luckily I won't miss it. Monuments are for the living not the dead. It would take at least a year to go through everyone in my head and say goodbye. I don't want to cry now. I'm glad I can look back without bitterness. The beautiful evenings with Melchior! – under the willows, the forester's hut, the old battleground with the five lime trees, the quiet ruins of the castle. When the moment comes I'll think with my whole being of whipped cream. Whipped cream won't stop me. It leaves behind a pleasant aftertaste, it doesn't end up in your trousers . . . And then I've always thought people were worse than they are. I've never met one who didn't try his best. I felt sorry for them because they had me to deal with. I go to the altar like an ancient Etruscan youth. His death rattles bring his brothers prosperity for the year ahead. Drop by drop I drink the dregs. The secret shudders of crossing

141

over. I weep with the sadness of my lot. Life gave me the cold shoulder. From the other side solemn, friendly faces beckon me: the headless queen, the headless queen – compassion, waiting for me, with open arms . . . The laws of this world are for children, I've earned my pass. The balance sinks, the butterfly rises and flies away. The painted veil no longer blinds me. Why should I play this mad game with illusion? The mists part! Life is a question of taste.

Translation by Edward Bond

COMMENTARY: Wedekind's *Spring Awakening* focuses on a group of adolescents as they awaken to their sexuality and come into inevitable conflict with their repressive parents and teachers. Wedekind sympathetically presents Moritz and his friends; with all their fears, delights and neuroses fully revealed. Almost like a painting, the play uses bold, colourful images to create a canvas of dreamlike urges and fantasies that touch an audience with their explicit honesty. Today, one hundred years after its first notorious performance, it still manages to provoke audiences with its frank portrayal of sexuality.

Moritz's monologue is like a look inside his head as he reaches a breaking point. This is a crisis for him and there will be no turning back. His brain is seething with frightened life. There are moments of great lucidity but much of what he says is more imagistic than coherent. The actor himself, however, must be in control at all times. Moritz tries to counter his childish emotions, especially the desire to cry, with adult language. One of the aims of the speech is that he is desperately *trying* to make sense of his feelings. Notice how calm and resolved he becomes once he begins to accept death. The last part of the speech is full of sacrificial drama with Moritz playing the willing victim. The actor must work with the imagery and the often consciously literary language to mirror the complex life and death emotions fighting within Moritz.

A Streetcar Named Desire
(1947) Tennessee Williams

Scene 7. The kitchen of an apartment building in New Orleans.

Stanley Kowalski is 'about twenty-eight or thirty years old, roughly dressed in blue denim work clothes. He is of medium height, about five feet eight or nine, and strongly, compactly built. Animal joy in his being is implicit in all his movements and attitudes. Since earliest manhood the centre of his life has been pleasure with women, the giving and taking of it, not with weak indulgence, dependently, but with the power and pride of a richly feathered male bird among hens. Branching out from this complete and satisfying centre are all the auxiliary channels of his life, such as his heartiness with men, his appreciation of rough humour, his love of good drink and food and games, his car, his radio, everything that is his, that bears his emblem of the gaudy seed-bearer. He sizes women up at a glance, with sexual classifications, crude images flashing into his mind and determining the way he smiles at them.' He is married to Stella. Her sister, Blanche comes to stay, and meets Stanley for the first time. Blanche is an ethereal, neurotic Southern lady who flaunts her genteel airs and graces. However, Stanley sees through her and decides to investigate some of Blanche's stories. He believes she has squandered Stella's rightful inheritance and wants his revenge. While Blanche is off having a bath, he confronts Stella who has resolutely refused to believe Stanley's accusations against her sister.

STANLEY. Honey, I told you I thoroughly checked on these stories! Now wait till I finish. The trouble with Dame Blanche was that she couldn't put on her act any more in Laurel! They got wised up after two or three dates with her and then they quit, and she goes on to another, the same old line, same old act, some old hooey! But the town was too

143

small for this to go on forever! And as time went by she became a town character. Regarded as not just different but downright loco – nuts. [STELLA *draws back*.] And for the last year or two she has been washed up like poison. That's why she's here this summer, visiting royalty, putting on all this act – because she's practically told by the mayor to get out of town! Yes, did you know there was an army camp near Laurel and your sister's was one of the places called 'Out-of-Bounds'?

[BLANCHE. 'It's only a paper moon, Just as phony as it can be –

But it wouldn't be make-believe If you believed in me!']

Well, so much for her being such a refined and particular type of girl. Which brings us to Lie Number Two.

[STELLA. I don't want to hear any more!]

She's not going back to teach school! In fact I am willing to bet you that she never had no idea of returning to Laurel! She didn't resign temporarily from the high school because of her nerves! No, siree, Bob! She didn't. They kicked her out of that high school before the spring term ended – and I hate to tell you the reason that step was taken! A seventeen-year-old boy – she'd gotten mixed up with!

[BLANCHE. 'It's a Barnum and Bailey world, Just as phoney as it can be – '

STELLA. This is making me – sick!]

The boy's old dad learned about it and got in touch with the high school superintendent. Boy, oh boy, I'd like to have been in that office when Dame Blanche was called on the carpet! I'd like to have seen her trying to squirm out of that one! But they had her on the hook good and proper that time and she knew that the jig was all up! They told her she better move on to some fresh territory. Yep, it was practickly a town ordinance passed against her!

COMMENTARY: Stanley Kowalski, in *A Streetcar Named Desire*, is undoubtedly the greatest male role in modern American drama. Actors as varied as Marlon Brando, Anthony Quinn and Alec Baldwin have played this tough, working-class man. Each of these actors found a unique way to convey Stanley's macho brio and savage spirit. Like all of Tennessee Williams' best heroes, Stanley is a truth speaker out to expose fakes. Blanche Dubois has invaded his home and set Stella against him. Stanley wants to get Blanche and nail her with the facts he has gathered.

Until this point in the play Stanley has been a man of few words. He dominates with his physique rather than with words. The actor should create a strong and active physical presence. He is a man whose personal comfort always comes first. He likes roaming around his own home bare-chested. Being articulate is not one of Stanley's strong points; brutal honesty is. He pummels Stella with the truth about her sister, punching home the wounding facts. He can see that Stella finds all this hard to stomach; it literally makes her sick. Stanley is relentless. He wants to make sure that Stella hears every piece of his evidence against Blanche. He comes at her from all sides until he is practically shouting the lines into her face. His words are full of contempt. Like a prosecution lawyer, Stanley's momentum increases with each point he scores. This is his chance to take sarcastic revenge on 'Dame' Blanche, the woman who called him an 'animal'. When all his suspicions about Blanche are confirmed the fury that has been growing throughout the play finally erupts and in his anger he finds a rough eloquence. Because there are so many revelations in this speech the actor has to guard himself from reaching a climax too soon. Although he is a man easily given to rage and physical violence, particularly when he drinks, the actor must remember that this outburst and resentment stems from his passionate belief that Stella has been wronged.

Table Manners

(1973) Alan Ayckbourn

Act 1, scene 2. A dining room. Sunday morning, 9 am.

Norman Dewers (30s) is a suburban assistant librarian and married to Ruth, an obsessive career-woman. His rather ordinary exterior belies the passionate Lothario with a roving eye lurking inside. Norman invites Annie, his sister-in-law, away for a secret dirty weekend and comes to pick her up at her mother's house. Annie's sister, however, discovers their plan and puts an end to it. Norman has to stay the night along with Annie, Sarah and her husband Reg. At breakfast the following morning, Norman is given a particularly frosty reception, provoking him into a comically confessional tirade that sends Sarah and Annie from the room. Alone with Reg, Norman (still in his pyjamas and with a bowl of cereal in his hand) explains his intentions.

NORMAN. Oh, well. It's a bit quieter without those two. Hear yourself speak. Too damned noisy before. All that crunching of toast. Like a brigade of Guards marching on gravel. Well now, Reg – (REG *chews glumly through his cereal. Looking round the table.*) Milk? Ah. (*He gets up.*) Sugar? (*He returns with these and sits. Pouring milk over his cereal.*) Nice peaceful morning. Just the two of us and – hark! the soft crackle of my Puffa Puffa rice. 'Tis spring indeed. (*Slight pause.*) I suppose you think I'm cruel too, don't you? Well, I've damn good cause to be, haven't I? I mean, nobody's thought about my feelings, have they? It's all Annie – Annie – Annie . . . what about me? I was going to give her everything. Well, as much, as I could. My whole being. I wanted to make her happy for a weekend, that's all. I wanted to give her . . . (*Angrily.*) It was only for a few

146

hours for God's sake. Saturday night, back on Monday morning. That was all it was going to be. My God! The fuss. What about your wife, Norman? What about my wife? Don't you think I'd take Ruth away, just the same? If she'd come. But she won't. She has no need of me at all, that woman, except as an emotional punch bag . . . I tell you, if you gave Ruth a rose, she'd peel all the petals off to make sure there weren't any greenfly. And when she'd done that, she'd turn round and say, do you call that a rose? Look at it, it's all in bits. That's Ruth. If she came in now, she wouldn't notice me. She'd probably hang her coat on me . . . It's not fair, Reg. Look, I'll tell you. A man with my type of temperament should really be ideally square jawed, broad shouldered, have blue twinkling eyes, a chuckle in his voice and a spring in his stride. He should get through three women a day without even ruffling his hair. That's what I'm like inside. That's my appetite. That's me. I'm a three a day man. There's enough of me in here to give. Not just sex, I'm talking about everything. The trouble is, I was born in the wrong damn body. Look at me. A gigolo trapped in a haystack. The tragedy of my life Norman Dewers – gigolo and assistant librarian. What's inside you, Reg? Apart from twelve bowls of cornflakes? What do you feel with Sarah? Do you sometimes feel like saying to her, no this is me. The real me. Look at me . . . (REG *finishes his cornflakes*.)

COMMENTARY: Ayckbourn's *Table Manners* (part of a trilogy of plays called *The Norman Conquests*) paradoxically finds high comedy in moments of poignant isolation. The play portrays a family with only marginal feelings for one another. Each character is entirely self-absorbed and concerned only with his or her own happiness and satisfaction. They all talk but rarely listen. Even during a major revelation, when a character is mournfully baring

147

his soul, no one hears him. Behind the surface of brilliant farce is a world of personal, marital and sexual frustration.

Norman is at the centre of the drama. His insatiable appetite for sexual 'conquest' is the catalyst that pushes the emotional pulse of the action faster and faster. The actor should relish the fact that the sexually charged Norman is not an Adonis, but just a shabby, woolly-hatted librarian. He is a manipulator and hypocrite who shifts allegiances at the drop of a cornflake. He loves nothing more than to have an audience for his rambling, woolly thoughts and endless jokes. He creates little scenarios with himself as the star. All the characters are wise to him and his ways. So wise, in fact, that they have stopped paying attention to his justifications. Yet Norman is masterful at acts of self-pity, he can wring a tear out of any sentence. Norman is also a loner – notice his numerous references to isolation. This is a speech that should be delivered at a leisurely, breakfast-time pace. In Reg, Norman has the perfect captive audience for his monologue.

The Tooth of Crime
(1972) Sam Shepard

Act 1. A bare stage except for an evil-looking black chair with silver studs and a very high back, something like an Egyptian Pharaoh's throne but simple, centre stage.

Hoss is one of the great rockers who 'should look like a mean Rip Torn but a little younger'. He is wearing 'black rocker gear with silver studs and black kid gloves'. The action takes place in a violent future; a generation or two after 'the big ones. Dylan, Jagger, Townsend'. There is a code of behaviour where each rock star ('Marker'), has his territories ('marks') which he and his gang defend with deadly force. Their tools are lovingly restored antique guns, cars and motor bikes. Hoss himself has been groomed, 'When we first landed you, you were a complete beast of nature. A sideways killer. Then we moulded and shaped you and sharpened you down to perfection because we saw in you a true genius killer. A killer to end them all. A killer's killer.' Hoss is beginning to have a 'doubt dose' about his prowess, his age and a system which is changing too quickly for him, 'There's no sense of tradition in the game no more. . . . No art involved. No technique, no finesse.' He is threatened by a Gypsy, a 'kid', who plays outside the rules, and is challenging his mark. Here he voices his fears.

HOSS. [Yeah.] Look at me now. Impotent. Can't strike a kill unless the charts are right. Stuck in my image. Stuck in a mansion. Waiting. Waiting for a kid who's probably just like me. Just like I was then. A young blood. And I gotta off him. I gotta roll him or he'll roll me. We're fightin' ourselves. Just like turnin' the blade on ourselves. Suicide, man. Maybe Little Willard was right. Blow your fuckin' brains out. The whole thing's a joke. Stick a gun in your fuckin' mouth and pull the trigger. That's what it's all about. That's what we're

149

doin'. He's my brother and I gotta kill him. He's gotta kill me. Jimmy Dean was right. Drive the fuckin' Spider till it stings ya' to death. Crack up your soul! Jackson Pollock! Duane Allman! Break it open! Pull the trigger! Trigger me! Trigger you! Drive it off the cliff! It's an open highway. Long and clean and deadly beautiful. Deadly and lonesome as a jukebox.

[DOC. Come on, Becky, let's leave him alone.

HOSS. Yeah. Right.] Alone. That's me. Alone. That's us. All fucking alone. All of us. So don't go off in your private rooms with pity in mind. Your day is comin'. The mark'll come down to you one way or the other.

[BECKY. You better rest, Hoss.]

Ya' know, you'd be OK Becky, if you had a self. So would I. Something to fall back on in a moment of doubt or terror or even surprise. Nothin' surprises me no more. I'm ready to take it all on. The whole shot. The big one. Look at the Doc. A slave. An educated slave. Look at me. A trained slave. We're all so pathetic it's downright pathetic. And confidence is just a hype to keep away the open-ended shakes. Ain't that the truth, Doc?

[DOC. I don't know.]

Right. Right. 'I don't know' is exactly right. Now beat it, both of ya' before I rip your fuckin' teeth out a' yer heads!! GO ON BEAT IT!!!

BECKY *and* DOC *exit.* HOSS *sits in his chair and stares out in front of him. He talks to himself, sometimes shifting voices from his own into an older man's.*

(*Old.*) All right, Hoss, this is me talkin'. Yer old Dad. Yer old fishin' buddy. We used to catch eels side by side down by the dump. The full moon lit up the stream and the junk. The rusty chrome flashin' across the marsh. The fireflies dancin' like a faraway city. They'd swallow the hook all the way down. You remember that? (*Himself.*) Yeah. Sure. (*Old.*)

OK. You're not so bad off. It's good to change. Good to feel your blood pump. (*Himself.*) But where to? Where am I going? (*Old.*) It don't matter. The road's what counts. Just look at the road. Don't worry about where it's goin'. (*Himself.*) I feel so trapped. So fucking unsure. Everything's a mystery. I had it all in the palm of my hand. The gold, the silver. I knew. I was sure. How could it slip away like that? (*Old.*) It'll come back. (*Himself.*) But I'm not a true Marker no more. Not really. They're all countin' on me. The bookies, the agents, the Keepers. I'm a fucking industry. I even affect the stocks and bonds. (*Old.*) You're just a man, Hoss. Just a man. (*Himself.*) Yeah, maybe you're right. I'm just a man.

COMMENTARY: Sam Shepard's *The Tooth of Crime* draws its form, style and content from the world of rock music. Rhythm and energy pulse through the play's hip, idiomatic language. Hoss is an ageing superstar, an Elvis Presley act-alike, with touches of a gunslinger straight out of a Western movie. Like all such stars his hold on the top is lonely and tenuous. As a new contender comes on the scene Hoss is a target waiting to be toppled.

Hoss is a master of performance styles. He easily moves from one posture to another as though he were playing a medley of songs. The actor has to transform into new modes whenever the writing demands a change, shifting into a new key. The lines themselves are like song lyrics with poetic reverberations. Hoss is a consciously lyrical character although a strong bass line keeps him very anchored to the stage. The direction of the monologue also suggests it is like a dying fall. Gradually in the speech Hoss loses vitality and spirit. He becomes his father, ageing and withering. Puncturing his own persona he finally sees himself as just a man.

Ubu Cuckolded
(*c.* 1892) Alfred Jarry

Act 5, scene 2. The house of Achras.

Pa Ubu (40s) is 'sometime King of Poland and Aragon, professor of pataphysics'. He is bombastic, huge, vain and stupid – a monstrous clown. He has arrived, uninvited, at the house of Achras, a retired professor of mathematics. Ubu proceeds to commandeer the house, moving in his family, his debraining machine and his faithful band of Palcontents. He believes his wife, Ma Ubu, has cuckolded him with an Egyptian and he is set on vengeance. In this scene Pa Ubu's uncontrollable jealousy leads him to conclude that the innocent Rebontier has also cuckolded him.

PA UBU. Horn of Ubu, Mister Rebontier, it's you, I don't doubt any longer, who came to my house to cuckold me, who mistakes my virtuous wife, in other words for a piss-pot. We shall find ourselves, one fine day, thanks to you, the father of an archaeopteryx or worse, which won't look at all like us! Basically, we are of the opinion that cuckoldry implies marriage and therefore a marriage without cuck-oldry has no validity. But for form's sake we have decided to punish him severely. Palcontents, knock him down for me! (*The* PALCONTENTS *belabour* REBONTIER.) Lights, please, and you, Sir, answer me. Am I a cuckold?
[REBONTIER. Owowow, owowowow!]
How disgusting. He can't reply because he fell on his head. His brain has doubtless received an injury to the Broca convolution, where the faculty of holding forth resides. This convolution is the third frontal convolution on the left as you go in. Ask the hall-porter . . . Excuse me, gentlemen, ask
152

any philosopher: 'This dissolution of the mind is caused by an atrophy which little by little invades the cerebral cortex, then the grey matter, producing a fatty degeneration and atheroma of the cells, tubes, and capillaries of the nerve-substance!' There's nothing to be done with him. We'll have to make do with twisting the nose and nears, with removal of the tongue and extraction of the teeth, laceration of the posterior, hacking to pieces of the spinal marrow and the partial or total spaghettification of the brain through the heels. He shall first be impaled, then beheaded, then finally drawn and quartered. After which the gentleman will be free, through our great clemency, to go and get himself hanged anywhere he chooses. No more harm will come to him, for I wish to treat him well.

Translation by Cyril Connolly

COMMENTARY: Alfred Jarry's *Ubu* plays are outrageous satires on cruelty, power and dictatorship. Jarry created a unique theatrical style which combined elements of tragedy, farce and the puppet play. Pa Ubu is a gross monster, part Macbeth and part Mr Punch, who tortures and kills at the slightest whim. He is the spirit of annihilation who coddles with one hand and crushes with the other. Jarry also created Ubu as the ultimate caricature of all the negative values and ambitions of bourgeois society. He is the common man inflated to grotesque proportions.

Everything Ubu does calls for outsize acting: his gestures, his mood swings, his verbosity are all extravagant. The actor may want to try using masks and costume to help him create this grotesque personality. Although Ubu is a murderous, vengeful clown he is also like the fake physicians you find in *commedia dell'arte*, silly yet artful in his ability to make complete twaddle sound coherent. In the midst of bashing someone's brains out he can stop to give a small nonsensical lecture on the anatomy of the brain. Ubu loves the sound of his own voice and spouts double-talk that masquerades as true learning. There are no values in Ubu's world. He lives by his instincts, moment by moment. The actor must try to capture the dangerous fact that everything about Ubu is completely unpredictable and random. Although there are few clues in the text you should still try to find a way to give Ubu a unique vocal and physical dimension. He is a dangerous pretender. If he is played too comically the performance will miss the menace inherent in the character. Like Hitler, Ubu is a morbid clown whose lunacy has tragic implications.

Who's Afraid of Virginia Woolf?
(1962) Edward Albee

Act 2, 'Walpurgisnacht'. The living room of a house on the campus of a small New England college. Night.

George (46) is thin with 'hair going grey'. He has been married to Martha, who is six years his senior, for over twenty years. He teaches History at the college run by Martha's father. They invite Nick and Honey, a new young faculty couple, over for drinks. By the time the guests arrive George and Martha have already had several drinks and are in a combative mood. As the evening wears on and alcohol takes its toll they become increasingly abusive towards one another. Nick and Honey become their victims too. George addresses this speech to everyone in the room.

GEORGE (*with great authority*). SILENCE! (*It is respected.*) Now, how are we going to play Get the Guests?
[MARTHA. For God's sake George. . . .
GEORGE. You be quiet! (MARTHA *shrugs.*)] I wonder. . . . I wonder. (*Puzzles . . . then. . . .*) OK! Well . . . Martha . . . in her indiscreet way . . . well, not really indiscreet, because Martha is a naive, at heart . . . anyway, Martha told you all about my first novel. True or false? Huh? I mean, true or false that there ever was such a thing. HA! But, Martha told you about it . . . my first novel, my . . . memory book . . . which I'd sort of preferred she hadn't, but hell, that's blood under the bridge. BUT! what she didn't do . . . what Martha didn't tell you about is she didn't tell us all about my *second* novel. (MARTHA *looks at him with puzzled curiosity.*) No, you didn't know about that,

did you, Martha? About my second novel, true or false. True or false?

[MARTHA (*sincerely*). No.]

No. (*He starts quietly but as he goes on, his tone becomes harsher, his voice louder.*) Well, it's an allegory, really – probably – but it can be read as straight cozy prose . . . and it's all about a nice young couple who come out of the middle west. It's a bucolic you see. AND, this nice young couple comes out of the middle west, and she's blonde and about thirty, and he's a scientist, a teacher, a scientist . . . and his mouse is a wifey little type who gargles brandy all the time . . . and . . .

[NICK. Just a minute here. . . .]

. . . and they got to know each other when they was only teensie little types, and they used to get under the vanity table and poke around, and . . .

[NICK. I said JUST A MINUTE!]

This is my game! You played yours . . . you people. This is my game!

[HONEY (*dreamy*). I want to hear the story. I love stories.
MARTHA. George, for heaven's sake. . . .]

AND! Mousie's father was a holy man, see, and he ran sort of a travelling clip joint, based on Christ and all those girls, and he took the faithful . . . that's all . . . just took 'em . . .

[HONEY (*puzzling*). This is familiar . . .
NICK (*voice shaking a little*). No kidding!]

. . . and he died eventually. Mousie's pa, and they pried him open, and all sorts of money fell out . . . Jesus money, Mary money . . . LOOT!

COMMENTARY: Albee's *Who's Afraid of Virginia Woolf?* is a powerful drama of confrontation. George and Martha are locked in a physically intense and emotionally violent love-hate relationship.

Alcohol fuels their caustic passions. Their innocent guests also become enmeshed in the psychological and pugilistic mind-games. As the evening wears on, the realities of the present and past truths are revealed and confronted. One by one their dreams and delusions are exposed and shattered.

George uses his guests to get at Martha. The enmity between husband and wife is intense and finds an outlet in theatrical charades. A cocktail party and polite conversations, for instance, are merely charades. George and Martha are expert at masking their real motives and personalities behind a barrier of civility. George's aim here is to strip away those masks of hypocrisy and expose naked motivations. His 'allegory' is clearly intended to discomfort Nick and Honey, and indirectly embarrass Martha. The actor, despite George's alcoholic buzz, must keep the story on track. At every moment George is playing to his onstage audience and notes their every reaction. Look at all the shifts George makes throughout the speech. When he is interrupted he only gets louder. The story he tells is morbidly grotesque and George takes glee in its black humour. The actor should remember not to indicate George's drunkenness, but should find a way to reveal the influence of the alcohol and not merely its effects.

Play Sources

Absent Friends by Alan Ayckbourn in *Three Plays* (Penguin)

All My Sons by Arthur Miller in *Miller Plays: One* (Methuen)

American Buffalo by David Mamet in *Mamet Plays: One* (Methuen)

Antigone by Jean Anouilh in *Anouilh: Five Plays* (Methuen)

Becket by Jean Anouilh (Methuen)

Bingo by Edward Bond in *Bond Plays: Three* (Methuen)

The Blood Knot by Athol Fugard in *Selected Plays* (Oxford University Press)

Blues for Mister Charlie by James Baldwin (Samuel French)

Caligula by Albert Camus in *Caligula and Other Plays* (Penguin)

The Caretaker by Harold Pinter (Faber)

The Caucasian Chalk Circle by Bertolt Brecht (Methuen)

Chips with Everything by Arnold Wesker in *Wesker Plays: Volume 3* (Penguin)

Cloud Nine by Caryl Churchill in *Churchill Plays: One* (Methuen)

Curse of the Starving Class by Sam Shepard in *Seven Plays* (Faber)

A Day in the Death of Joe Egg by Peter Nichols in *Nichols Plays: One* (Methuen)

East by Steven Berkoff (Faber)

Entertaining Mr Sloane by Joe Orton in *Orton: The Complete Plays* (Methuen)

Faith Healer by Brien Friel in *Selected Plays* (Faber)

The Glass Menagerie by Tennessee Williams (Penguin)

The Homecoming by Harold Pinter (Faber)

The House of Blue Leaves by John Guare (Samuel French & Methuen)

Huis Clos [No Exit/In Camera] by Jean-Paul Sartre in *In Camera and Other Plays* (Penguin)

The Iceman Cometh by Eugene O'Neill (Nick Hern Books)

Krapp's Last Tape by Samuel Beckett (Faber)

La Turista by Sam Shepard in *Seven Plays* (Faber)

Long Day's Journey into Night by Eugene O'Neill (Nick Hern Books)

Look Back in Anger by John Osborne (Faber)

The Maids by Jean Genet in *The Maids: with Deathwatch* (Faber)

Murder in the Cathedral by T. S. Eliot (Faber)

Napoli Milionaria by Eduardo de Filippo in *De Filippo: Four Plays* (Methuen)

The Night of the Iguana by Tennessee Williams (Penguin)

Otherwise Engaged by Simon Gray (Faber)

Present Laughter by Noël Coward in *Coward Plays: Four* (Methuen)

The Price by Arthur Miller in *Miller Plays: Two* (Methuen)

Pygmalion by Bernard Shaw (Penguin)

The Resistible Rise of Arturo Ui by Bertolt Brecht in *Brecht Plays: Three* (Methuen)

Rhinoceros by Eugène Ionesco in *Plays: Volume 4* (John Calder)

Rosencrantz and Guildenstern are Dead by Tom Stoppard (Faber)

The Rules of the Game by Luigi Pirandello in *Pirandello: Three Plays* (Methuen)

The Ruling Class by Peter Barnes in *Barnes Plays: One* (Methuen)

Sexual Perversity in Chicago by David Mamet in *Mamet Plays: One* (Methuen)

Spring Awakening by Frank Wedekind (Methuen)

A Streetcar Named Desire by Tennessee Williams (Penguin)

Table Manners (The Norman Conquests) by Alan Ayckbourn in *The Norman Conquests* (Penguin)

The Tooth of Crime by Sam Shepard in *Seven Plays* (Faber)

Ubu Cuckolded by Alfred Jarry in *The Ubu Plays* (Methuen)

Who's Afraid of Virginia Woolf? by Edward Albee (Penguin)

Acknowledgements

The editors and publishers gratefully acknowledge permission to reproduce copyright material in this book:

Edward Albee: from *Who's Afraid of Virginia Woolf?* Copyright © 1962 by Edward Albee. Reprinted by permission of Jonathan Cape. Jean Anouilh: from *Antigone*, trans. Barbara Bray. Copyright © 1987 by Jean Anouilh and Barbara Bray. From *Becket*, trans. Lucienne Hill. Copyright © 1960 by Jean Anouilh and Lucienne Hill. Both reprinted by permission of Methuen London. Alan Ayckbourn: from *Absent Friends*. Copyright © 1977 by Alan Ayckbourn. First published by Chatto and Windus in *Three Plays* (1977). From *Table Manners*. Copyright © 1975 by Alan Ayckbourn. First published by Chatto and Windus in *The Norman Conquests*. All reprinted by permission of Chatto and Windus and Grove Press, Inc. James Baldwin: from *Blues for Mister Charlie*. Copyright © 1964 by James Baldwin. Reprinted by permission of Bantam Doubleday Dell Publishing Group, Inc. Peter Barnes: from *The Ruling Class*. Copyright © 1969, 1989 by Peter Barnes. Reprinted by permission of Methuen London. Samuel Beckett: from *Krapp's Last Tape*. Copyright © 1958 by Samuel Beckett. Reprinted by permission of Faber and Faber Ltd and Grove Press Inc. Steven Berkoff: from *East*. Copyright © 1977, 1978 by Steven Berkoff. Reprinted by permission of Faber and Faber Ltd. Edward Bond: from *Bingo*. Copyright © 1974 by Edward Bond. First published in 1974 by Eyre Methuen Ltd. Reprinted by permission of Methuen London. Bertolt Brecht: from *The Resistible Rise of Arturo Ui*, trans. Ralph Manheim. Translation copyright © 1981 by Stefan S. Brecht. Original work entitled *Der aufhaltsame Aufstieg des Arturo Ui*. Copyright © 1957 by Suhrkamp Verlag, Berlin. From *The Caucasian Chalk Circle*, trans. Ralph Manheim. Translation copyright © 1976 by Stefan S. Brecht. Original work entitled *Der kaukasische Kreiderderkreis*. Copyright © 1955 by Suhrkamp Verlag, Berlin. All reprinted by permission of Methuen London. Caryl Churchill: from *Cloud Nine*. Copyright © 1979 by Caryl

The editors and publishers have made all possible effort to assure the accuracy of the facts used in this book, and to make the text as comprehensible as possible. They cannot, however, assume responsibility for any errors, and should communicate them to the publisher.

CAUTION: The authors are not necessarily responsible for the content of this book, and should be consulted before any action is taken that might result in personal injury. The editors and publishers specifically disclaim any responsibility for any loss or risk incurred as a consequence of the use and application of any of the contents of this book.